What
MENNONITES
Are
THINKING
–2001–

What
MENNONITES
Are
THINKING
–2001–

— Edited by —
Merle Good *and*
Phyllis Pellman Good

Good Books

Intercourse, PA 17534
800/762-7171
www.goodbks.com

Design by Dawn J. Ranck

WHAT MENNONITES ARE THINKING, 2001

Copyright © 2001 by Good Books, Intercourse, PA 17534

International Standard Book Number: 1-56148-323-0
ISSN: 1099-0704

This book is made possible
in part by the following sponsors—

Eastern Mennonite University

The People's Place

Mennonite Weekly Review

Goshen College

Good Books

*(Please read the sponsors' messages
on pages 285-290)*

Acknowledgments

"Thoughts on Finding a Home and Staying There" by Bethany Spicher is reprinted by permission from *Crossroads* (Spring 2001), of Eastern Mennonite University.

"What Makes a Mennonite Leader? One Ethiopian Mennonite's Point of View" by Phyllis Pellman Good is reprinted by permission from *Courier* (Number 2, 2001), of Mennonite World Conference.

"Naming Sin and Communicating Compassion" by Ronald J. Sider is reprinted by permission from *PRISM Magazine* (July/August 2000).

"Shaken Security" by James M. Sensenig is reprinted by permission from *The Eastern Mennonite Testimony* (Volume XXXIII, October, 2001).

"God's Spirit and a Theology for Living" by David Kline is reprinted by permission of The Johns Hopkins University Press from Redekop, Calvin, ed. *Creation and the Environment: An Anabaptist Perspective on a Sustainable World,* pp. 61-69. © 2000.

"Surprised" by Sarah Klassen is reprinted by permission from *Sophia* (Volume 10, Number 1, Spring 2000).

"Green Man in Good Neighborhood" by Rhoda Janzen first appeared in *New Scriblerus* (September 2001).

"Table Prayer" by Keith Ratzlaff was first published in *The Georgia Review* (Spring 2000).

"Rhapsody with Dark Matter" by Jeff Gundy is reprinted by permission from *Rhapsody with Dark Matter: Poems,* courtesy of Bottom Dog Press. © 2000.

"Markings" is from *Tasting the Dust,* by Jean Janzen, © 2000. Reprinted by permission of Good Books.

WHAT MENNONITES ARE THINKING, 2001

Acknowledgments

The book review by John W. Miller of *God's Healing Strategy; An Introduction to the Bible's Main Themes* and *How To Understand the Bible* is reprinted by permission from *Canadian Mennonite* (June 18, 2001).

The book review by Lori Matties of *Tasting the Dust* is reprinted by permission from *The Journal of Mennonite Studies,* 19 (2001).

The book review by Joseph A. Sprunger of *The Hammer Rings Hope: Photos and Stories from Fifty Years of Mennonite Disaster Service* is reprinted by permission from *Pennsylvania Mennonite Heritage* (April 2001), of the Lancaster (PA) Mennonite Historical Society.

The book review by John A. Lapp of *Anabaptist Visions for the New Millennium: A Search for Identity* is reprinted by permission from *Mennonite Weekly Review* (May 10, 2001).

The book review by Valerie G. Rempel of *Calling God "Father": Essays on the Bible, Fatherhood, and Culture* is reprinted by permission from *The Conrad Grebel Review* (Winter 2001).

The book review by Ann Hostetler of *Dangerous Elements* and *Simone Weil: Songs of Hunger and Love* is reprinted by permission from *The Mennonite Quarterly Review,* 75 (January 2001).

Table of Contents

Introduction

We are pleased to present our fourth annual collection for your consideration and enjoyment. Our goal has been to create an annual, containing some of the best current Mennonite writing and thinking.

"Mennonite" can mean faith, as accepted by certain groups of Christians who claim that name (Amish and Brethren are related groups). "Mennonite" can also bring to mind any of a variety of ways of life. This conversation/tension between faith and life forms the backdrop for many of the pieces in this collection.

Writings were selected on the basis of both content and style. For many pieces, this marks their first publication. All others, to qualify, were published since January 1, 1999.

Writers were eligible if they: a) are current members of a Mennonite-related group, or b) have had a significant interaction of many years with a Mennonite-related group, or c) deal with Mennonite-related material in a compelling way.

Please note that the Cumulative Indexes beginning on page 291 include both this year's collection, as well as *What Mennonites Are Thinking, 1998, What Mennonites Are Thinking, 1999,* and *What Mennonites Are Thinking, 2000.* (Copies of any of these three books may be ordered from your local bookstore or by calling 800/762-7171. Note the special order form at the back of this book.)

We hope readers of many backgrounds will enjoy this volume, including readers among our various Mennonite-related groups.

—Merle Good and Phyllis Pellman Good, Editors

Featured Articles,
Essays, and Opinions, I

A Retired Jesus?

by C. Norman Kraus

Some years ago I was asked to address a group of my retired colleagues from the teaching faculty of Goshen College. We were gathering to enjoy a "retired faculty retreat" in the place where we had often met as an active faculty to prepare for the approaching year of study and teaching. I could pick my topic.

The motto, *"Nachfolge Christi,"* had been our guiding principle in our vocation as Christian college teachers. Now most of us were in a retirement mode, collecting our Social Security and whatever retirement funds that had accrued, and we were free to do what we liked. Indeed, it was precisely that freedom from scheduled responsibilities that made it possible to meet while younger colleagues were at work.

As I pondered what subject to reflect upon, I thought of how the *Nachfolge Christi* motto applied to our lives as "old people." Jesus was a young social activist who ended up a martyr soon after the age of 30. He was even younger than Martin Luther King, whom many of us had admired, when he died. And in our Anabaptist tradition it did not help that most of our heroes were young people who were martyred at an early age.

Could I imagine Jesus being old and retired? If not, how did his life example relate to our life in retirement?

I raised the question with several of my colleagues. "Can you imagine a retired Jesus?" One responded with a cautious, "I'm wondering what you have in mind." Another said flatly, "No." A third opined that "Martyrs don't retire." And yet a fourth venerable theologian referred to the "absurdity" of the very idea. But if it is so absurd to think of Jesus as retired, then what are we, who made such a point of following his life and example, doing living in relatively affluent ease with the goal of enjoying the fruits of our hard work?

This turned my mind to the opposite side of the question. When did "old people" begin to be "senior citizens" and "retirees"? *Grosseltern* didn't retire. They continued to be part of the life of the extended family. How did we get from the *Grossdadt Haus* to Social Security, retirement funds, and retirement villas? And what are the implications for our lives as Christians? How do we apply the biblical, and more particularly the New Testament, teaching of and about Jesus to this new social phenomena?

One weakness of our western Christian culture is its lack of a positive spiritual vision for old people. Even the Bible does not give us an idealized view of old age as a time of spiritual fruition. Since in our modern society we tend to associate virtue with work, retirement is viewed as the deserved reward for work. Thus, even in Christian circles, the AARP picture of material security and personal enjoyment idealizes the "senior years" as a time of enjoying deferred material pleasure.

The Hebrew picture from the Old Testament suggests that old age is a time to enjoy the fruit of a lifetime of labor, but at the same time it is a time of increasing vulnerability and dependence on children. If one makes it to 70, at most 80, one can expect only toil and trouble (Psalm 90:10; Ecclesiastes 12:1ff).

The Levitical requirements for vows to be paid to the temple recognize the years between 20 and 60 as the productive time of life, and for those above 60 the amount required is significantly reduced (Leviticus 27:1-8).

The aging years are a time of dependence, and children are to care for ("honor") their old parents. Even in the New Testament one gets much the same picture. Jesus strongly criticized the rabbinical law of "Corban" which provided a loophole to this responsibility of children (Mark 7:10-13).

This is in contrast, for example, to Hinduism's view of the stages (ashrama) of life culminating in a time for meditation and reflection upon the meaning of life. The ideal life progresses toward a world of spiritual fulfillment. After an active life, the aging person, that is, 55 and above, should retire from the distractions of business and home life and go to a place (ashram) where the mind can be focused on the really important dimensions of the spirit. The goal is to become free of worldly attachments and attractions, to become a spiritual parent to the oncoming generations. On the surface, at least, the biblical picture of the goal of earthly life is more materialistic.

So what is the significance of the example of Jesus for people in their aging years? Perhaps our clue is to be found in the resurrected Christ. The only New Testament picture of Jesus as an aged and ageless figure is found in Revelation 1:12-16. There he is pictured in an imposing vision with snow-white hair, bright penetrating eyes, legs and feet of an athlete, and a strong resonant voice. This is the picture of the Christ beyond death—the unchanging changing one, "the Alpha and

Omega, the beginning and the end." As the changeless one, he is at the same time infinitely adaptable and available to human need.

This one, who suffered all the pain, disappointment, misunderstanding, and shame that life could throw at him, and remained faithful to his calling is the savior of the world. In and through the resurrection, Jesus the Martyr is transformed into Jesus the Savior. And it is this one who calls us to take up the cross and follow his pattern for life in the confidence that we shall be like him in his resurrection.

While we cannot take the earthly Jesus as a literal ideal for our aging years, this does not mean that his example and teaching have no relevance for those 65 and over. The spiritual pattern and values by which he lived are timeless and timely. Certainly his words in Matthew 6:25ff about the need for daily trust in God's gracious sustenance have heightened meaning as we become increasingly vulnerable and dependent. And in a culture which glorifies physical existence and has a pagan view of death, his insistence on the importance of being reconciled to our mortality, and looking beyond death for the ultimate meaning of life, is pivotal. This is not a call to escape this life, but to view its importance in the perspective of eternity.

In a culture that equates "work" with labor for monetary gain, the call of Jesus in our retirement is a call to our true vocation. Like him we are called to "work the works of God who sent him [and us] (John 9:4). Our precise activities may change with retirement from positions in the national economy, but that does not negate the call to discipleship. Indeed, retirement may offer new possibilities for it. For example, I think of friends in Hokkaido who have used their new freedom from the pressures of professional jobs to join their daughter and family in establishing a truck farming model that can become the basis of a Christian retirement community.

And finally, Jesus' word that life does not consist of the things which we possess (Luke 12:15) must have special relevance for those of us retiring in a consumers' society, where the "good life" is defined as an affluent lifestyle. We are bombarded by the blandishment of consumerism and tempted to find our fulfillment in a AARP lifestyle. But both Jesus and Paul teach clearly that true satisfaction in life is found in spiritual accomplishments, not in material pleasures, and security is found in trusting relationships, not in stock market investments.

I have a friend who shortly after his retirement at 65 said, "I don't want to quit. I don't want to die on the vine!" And knowing what we do about Jesus, I suspect that he would not have died on the vine either. It is difficult to imagine him growing portly, settling for haute cuisine, ski slopes, and charter cruises. On the other hand, I expect that he would have retired from dominance on the active scene in the spirit of the Johannine Christ, who told his disciples that it was good for them that he was leaving his position of command.

C. Norman Kraus is a retired professor and theologian living in Harrisonburg, Virgina.

Thoughts on Finding a Home and Staying There

by Bethany Spicher

I think of all the homes I've known in my life.
Growing up in an Arizona city, I'd fall asleep every
night while my mother read poems, my dad
strummed hymns, and they both told stories about
their homes in Pennsylvania, until I believed that
green state was the promised land and this desert was
the wilderness.

And the Bible—for years we read it like a story-
book, a chapter an evening, straight through horrible
Leviticus and the strange Song of Solomon. And there
were always stories around the dinner table—from
Mennonite service workers on furlough, Amish relatives on vacations west and once the Eastern
Mennonite University (EMU) president on a fundrais-
ing trip.

When I was 12, we moved to Pennsylvania, met
our cousins, and rented a farm. We learned to milk
cows, pick stones, pull weeds, and stack bales; we
learned not to cry for the bull calves and to be glad
for rain; but it was not the promised land, it was hard
work. Something must have stuck, though, because
suddenly I was studying international agriculture at
EMU and then taking a year off for Mennonite
Voluntary Service in Kansas. Here, I met farmers who

have loved the same acres for decades, who get excited about vegetables, compost, beneficial insects, and rotational grazing, who know the injustice that comes with corporate agriculture and work for change by staying home in their own rural communities.

I came back to EMU preaching sustainable ag, denouncing the cafeteria for California lettuce and Guatemala grapes, vowing to plow up the soccer fields and build a barn beside the University Commons. I thought my friends would join me, but, just home from Nicaragua, the West Bank, Australia, they had campaigns of their own, stories about migrant workers, political prisoners, and indigenous people that made my small farmers look like oppressors. We all talked at once, showing pictures, explaining histories, translating foreign words, until, sobered by tests and papers, we set to work connecting our stories to the rest of our lives.

Faith, I think, is a choice, like a house that you build and live in, like a garden you plant and eat from. Having grown up with bedtime stories, homegrown tomatoes, and Jesus in my heart, I didn't have to tear down any walls, dig up any foundations to reconstruct my house. (Some of my friends did; it's hard work.)

It was like adding windows and skylights when I noticed that the Bible includes creation, the year of jubilee, the parables with their seeds, soil, and farmers; when I understood that the Jesus in me is also the one in all things, before all things, the one who holds everything together—from spinning atoms to the widening universe to the crazy, conflicting church.

Thoughts on Finding a Home and Staying There

On the verge of graduation, I'm brimming with
plans—traveling the world, buying a farm, founding
a non-profit, reversing desertification in sub-Saharan
Africa, removing all the land mines from the fertile
fields of southeast Asia, and coming back to single-
handedly unite the Mennonite Church USA.

I'm learning, though, that only Jesus can hold
everything together, that not even Menno Simons
could be all things to all people, and that I have
friends who will do good work, too.

So, as for me, I'll choose a town in Pennsylvania, a
block in D.C., a village in Angola or China to love,
and then settle in for a season, tell some stories,
plant some seeds, stay at home.

*Bethany Spicher, Huntingdon, Pennsylvania, graduated
from Eastern Mennonite University with a major in international agriculture.*

What Makes
a Mennonite Leader?
One Ethiopian Mennonite's Point of View
by Phyllis Pellman Good

Consider the fact that the President of Mennonite World Conference (MWC) grew up in a family that practiced Confucianism and ancestor worship, and that MWC's Vice President was raised a Muslim. What makes a leader in the Mennonite world today? Apparently not the length—nor the entanglement—of one's roots in a Mennonite family tree.

Bedru Hussein of Ethiopia, now in his fourth year as Vice President of Mennonite World Conference, carries three striking qualities—a giant stillness that is almost tangible, a view of leadership that bears consideration, and a coming-to-Christ that one might be tempted to call an accident.

"My parents were very ardent Muslims," he explains. And so they raised him to be as well. From them he learned that what one believes, one lives. "My parents were very pious; they held monthly religious meetings in our home. My father was also recruited as a soldier."

Believing that their son was securely fixed in their Muslim faith, Bedru's parents sent him at the age of five to an Orthodox priests' school so he would have a better education. "There I was introduced to the Lord's Prayer and the Ten Commandments." Somewhere between his Muslim upbringing and his brush with Christianity, Bedru remembers that "I began to want to thank God. And there was a low voice that I heard, urging me to keep the Ten Commandments."

One day on the playground during recess, a handful of paper fragments swirled over 13-year-old Bedru's feet. One of the torn papers particularly attracted his attention. "On it, in English, was part of the rich young ruler's story. Who is Jesus, I began to wonder. My classmates tried to explain a lot to me, but they couldn't seem to answer that question to my satisfaction."

Despite the displeasure of his family, Bedru continued his curiosity about Christianity through his teen years and into his university training. A Billy Graham film and University Christian Students' Fellowship brought him to a confession of Christian faith in 1966 when he was 18.

"I was part of the Ethiopian revival; the Lord was raising up Christians at that time. But hand-in-hand with that action was another by a group of students who were forming a Communist party. The two movements grew simultaneously."

A Developing View of Leadership

From the beginning of his involvement with the Christian church, Bedru and his Christian compatriots realized that the work of the church could not be left primarily in the hands of a few select leaders.

There were too many demands, too many needs, too many expectations. Teachers of the gospel were needed on university campuses where interest in a new approach to life was at a peak. But teachers were also in demand throughout the entire country where the church was growing and spreading. "When both students and faculty returned to their homes, they needed well prepared churches to join," observes Bedru.

Education has been his burden ever since. "Not all pastoral gifts can be in one person," he states emphatically. "The only way the church can grow is to involve all lay members." But preparation of church members has not been left to chance among Ethiopian Mennonites, with whom Bedru affiliated after he was hired as a teacher by a Mennonite high school in 1976.

Not only was he an instructor in biology for six years in that school, but he began teaching "apologetics, especially to young people of Mennonite and other denominations." In that mix of professional and religious activity, Bedru demonstrated an ideal that has become a hallmark of the Meserete Kristos Church (MKC). "Members participate in every aspect of church life. Wherever an MKC member goes, he or she becomes a leader," Bedru explains. "It's part of the culture of our church life.

"We believe in team leadership. And we believe in freeing the lay members. They are all 'priests'; each has a gift."

The exercise of those gifts, however, is not left to chance. A careful system is in place to nudge members toward the areas where they can be most useful. Bedru, who acknowledges that his own abilities and experience lie in administration and teaching, helped to hatch the methods for involving everyone in particular responsibilities within the church.

After 13 years as a biology teacher in one church school and two government schools, Bedru spent seven years as Executive Secretary of the Meserete Kristos Church. The experience as a church executive made him face the Ethiopian Mennonites' desperate need for trained pastors and leaders. In 1994, the Meserete Kristos College opened about 25 miles outside Addis Ababa, on the slope of a hillside where the city is fast approaching. At this point, courses are offered at a variety of levels in biblical and theological studies, especially for pastors and evangelists. The college's master plan calls for developing a Liberal Arts program, offering degrees in science, business administration, computer technology, nursing, and pharmacology.

The formation of this major institution prompted Bedru himself to head back to school, this time in North America. In the fall of 1997, he said goodbye to his wife, Kelemework Belete, and his four half-grown children and enrolled in Eastern Mennonite Seminary's three-year Master of Divinity program. His studies "shaped my conceptualization of things, not just to go forward, but to see in all directions. I wanted to be introduced to the tools of theology and to add a level to what I had already experienced in the church."

Bedru is now back in Ethiopia, appointed as Associate Principal of the Meserete Kristos College and teaching courses in leadership, administration, and missions.

Leaders who leave their country for extended training in another culture, and then return home, have to deal with re-entry. So, too, do their home communities. Bedru spent most of each summer in Ethiopia while he was studying in the States for three years, and he and his family established regular times for a monthly phone call during the school year. But the strain can't be completely avoided. "Some persons may be hesitant; they may think I'm liberal for having studied in the States. But my convictions are the same, although my approach may now be somewhat different," he comments.

Ethiopian Mennonites Train Other Christians, Too

The college is being noticed by other Christian groups. "We have some students from the Coptic Orthodox renewal movement," says Bedru. "We train them to return to their own churches." But MK College doesn't hide its particular emphases. "We have a peace stand. And that is part of our training for everyone. But we don't take sheep from other churches. We urge those leaders to stay in their churches. We can't make the whole church MKC!"

Nor does he want to. He speaks of a "laxity" within the MKC and of an effort on the part of leadership to have membership and attendance requirements become more vigorous. "We have an open meeting on Sunday and cell group meetings once a week. Those who don't attend are followed up on."

Bedru's years in North America gave him a close view of the Anabaptist-Mennonite churches there. "There is an individualistic attitude, but also a pluralistic attitude," he reflects. "People seem to think 'maybe this idea is good and that idea is good, and Jesus is one of many options.'

"Church work is put heavily on the pastor. People are too busy to develop relationships. Pastors are kept on the move; people want something new; they seem to want entertainers rather than serious Bible teachers."

The Pastor's Proper Part

He speaks softly but with firm conviction about what he believes are appropriate ways for the church to accomplish its tasks. "I think the Lord has given people to the church—and each has a gift—and they are all needed. A pastor can't have them all. A pastor can mobilize these gifts.

"Pastors should present themselves to God; ask to sense the peoples' hearts; look for people who can be leaders; spend time with them; discover the Bible together; fellowship together; train the laity; fast and pray together; involve all in church life. The pastor's task is to mobilize." It is a theme with him. "Pastors ought to engage members in a meaningful way so they can experience the visiting of the Spirit."

This Ethiopian leader explains the energy and boldness of his faith as a result of his "exposure to the baptism of the Holy Spirit." But he also thinks like an executive. "Too often there is no connection between seminary teaching—and congregations. People without a calling come to seminary. They can't quote Scriptures, but they come because they have the mental capacity. For some it's a profession. They market themselves in seminary.

"If churches want to grow, they need to mentor young people from their congregations, visit them when they go away to school or work, bond with them, call them back to leadership."

The strategy appears to be working. "The majority of our members are young people. We attract a lot of college students. We have a minister in Addis who cares for members who are in college. Every year we have 30-40 college students who become church leaders."

A Practical Proposal

When he's not deep into educational strategizing, Bedru dreams about Anabaptist-Mennonite churches from scattered places around the globe having intentional and meaningful interchange. "Why not have training institutes where Anabaptist-Mennonites from the Southern hemisphere and the Northern hemisphere come together to work at practical theology— living, working, praying, studying, doing research together. That kind of training would keep the Anabaptist identity clear, especially as we would study together. It would help to focus our identity.

"How about sending North American seminary profs to satellite training centers around the world for short periods of time? That would certainly enrich their teaching when they return home.

"We're hoping that our Bible college can begin accepting students from North America. And I'm also working on having Eastern Mennonite Seminary [in Harrisonburg, Virginia] professors come to Ethiopia to teach on their sabbaticals. If they do, their lives will be different; their teaching will be changed.

"We need the North, and the North needs the South. We can talk to each other when we get together in big meetings, but doing together brings changes of attitude; it strengthens the bond in all directions."

His Essential Practices

How does Bedru maintain his energy and faith when resources lag so mercilessly behind the needs in Ethiopia? Those who have been his roommates at Mennonite World Conference meetings comment about his consistent discipline of rising early for several hours of prayer each morning. "I have prayer time for myself alone in the morning and before I go to bed. I read the Scriptures," he says simply. "Almost every day I get a message about what I should think about that day."

The Ethiopian Mennonites, and the global Anabaptist-Mennonite family, are the richer for having Bedru among them—with his broad worldview and his passion for mentoring all church members.

Phyllis Pellman Good, Lancaster, Pennsylvania, is a writer, editor, and co-editor of this collection.

Creativity and Obstacles

by Sandra Z. Richardson

A friend was telling me of a conversation she had with another friend. When she told him that she no longer believed in God, he responded with a question, "Oh, which God is that?"

Within Christianity there are different ways of looking at God. Whom we see depends on our perspective—where we are looking from—our history, our upbringing, our experiences. Maybe God does not change (which I sometimes doubt when reading certain Bible stories), but humans definitely change. I believe our changes influence the way we perceive God.

When I was a youth, I remember having a revelation about how we see God differently and that no one person can see all of God. The church youth group that I was a part of was sitting around a campfire in the woods behind my parents' house. I realized that what I was seeing in the fire—the ashes and the wood burning, perhaps the coals forming the changing image of the face of a tiger—all that, was not visible to someone sitting on the opposite side of the fire, or even to someone sitting three feet from me. What they saw, I could not see but had to trust their description. And maybe they didn't "see" anything. Maybe their strongest impression of the fire was its heat or the rhythm of its sound. But we could each share what we perceived and experienced of the fire from our own unique perspective. Together we could learn to appreciate the whole fire and its properties.

So which God am I talking about? What is my perspective? I am a visual artist. Perhaps the image of God I most understand and am drawn to is God as creator. "In the beginning God created . . . ," and it was good, but it didn't take long for things to go awry. We're not even out of chapter 3 of Genesis before Adam and Eve are banned from the garden. By chapter 4 the first murder has taken place, and by chapter 6 things are so bad, God is sorry he started the whole thing and is about to wipe it all out.

This seems to be the creative process in a nutshell: original inspiration and a plan, or at least a direction, we set out in; then the implementation of that plan. And then, something unexpected comes up, an obstacle of some sort that keeps us from our goal. The way is not clear; we make a mark we cannot erase; the work seems to take on a life of its own and goes in directions we did not anticipate; we have to make a decision and we choose the wrong one; we can't see where to go next.

Or the piece is just plain gutless, boring, flat. At that point we are tempted to throw it all in the trash, close the studio door, and get a real job.

But we don't do that. We don't give up. And neither did God. The rest of the Old Testament is the story of God discovering and preparing a way, of fanning the flames of justice, love, and forgiveness. Eventually that culminated in God taking on the limitations of human flesh and inserting himself into human history in the person of Jesus Christ.

Resolution. The final step of the creative process. If we stay with it through the frustration and despair, through the disgust and whining, through the unknown, through the foundering, eventually something comes. Often all of that makes a better, stronger piece than we originally had in mind. To get there, we must be willing to relinquish our original idea and, to some degree, control. And we need faith in the process.

What is faith in the process? It is a belief that there is a resolution, and that if we wait and have eyes to see and ears to hear, that the resolution will come. And when it does come, it can be exhilarating.

Ninety-five percent of working can be routine, boring, or tedious: showing up, putting one coil on top of the other, one letter beside another. But that five percent of the time when it all comes together, when we connect, when we make the piece sing, that is what keeps us going.

Bear in mind that this, of course, is a simplified version of the creative process, a formula. We all love formulas because they don't require us to think; we can just follow directions. The creative process is rarely so neatly linear as I have described. We don't necessarily work through something and wind up on the other side and that's it, all neat and tidy. It's easy to paint yourself into a corner with words.

So how does all of this talk of the creative process translate into how most of us live our lives? I believe as Christians we are called to live creatively. Things happen that muck up a lot, that make life complicated, that keep us from reaching our full potential. It may be divorce, depression, cancer, poverty, or boredom. It may be a consuming career or home life. We all seem to have something. For me, the major thing is *MS,* multiple sclerosis, that showed up in my life officially 10 years ago. A little aside here about the question of which God I believe in. The God I believe in did not cause my MS to happen, he did not bring this into my life as a trial, a lesson, an example, a punishment. It just happened. Now, what am I going to do? Frederick Buechner puts it best in his book *Telling Secrets.* He says:

> As I see it . . . God acts in history, and your and my brief histories, not as the puppeteer who sets the scene and works the strings but rather as the great director who, no matter what role fate casts us in, conveys to us, somehow, from the wings, if we have our eyes, ears, and hearts open and sometimes even if we don't, how we can play those roles in a way to enrich and ennoble and hallow the whole drama of things, including our own small but crucial parts in it.

MS has made life more complicated; even doing simple things has become progressively more difficult. This last year or so my disability seems to be accelerating. Over the years I have accepted into my life devices that have aided in mobility: first a cane, then a wheeled walker, hand controls in my car, now occasionally a wheelchair. I have accepted help from my husband, Stan, when my energy is flagging, for dressing and undressing. He washes my hair. Friends bring us meals. We have hired someone to clean the house.

Perhaps more difficult than these adjustments in my personal routine are the changes that my disability has brought in doing my artwork.

This was not the way I thought my life would go. So now what? If I approach my life as part of the creative process that I just described, then there is room, there is place for despair and for hope.

It is tempting to rush through or ignore the despair part, the part of the creative process where things go wrong, and to try to force a creative resolution. I believe it is important to take my time here, to grieve losses, to be sad, angry, depressed. Going back to the biblical account, I think it took God some time to work through his distress and anger when his creation took a different, unexpected turn.

Is it possible to recognize and experience despair and hope simultaneously? Perhaps that is what the creative process facilitates. As dark as things have gotten at times for me, hope stays by my side. It waits patiently through my tears, hands me a Kleenex. Stands beside me while we stand together on the edge, looking down into the depths of despair. Puts a hand on my shoulder that keeps me from falling.

Eventually, we return home. The tears subside. Then, recognizing the loss, acknowledging the deficits that remain, I start to think about how I can continue, what changes and adjustments I can make, what my options are.

For my artwork, that has meant hiring an assistant. At first I hired people to roll tiles, paint the colored glazes onto the surfaces of my pieces, move things from here to there. That left me more energy for the more creative parts of the process, like building or carving pieces. As my disability progresses, especially as it impacts arm and hand movement, I have had to consider ways to involve someone in these stages, too. This is more challenging.

It is during the building and carving phases that a piece evolves, that I bond with a piece. I may do sketches or a small model of a piece from which I catch a thread of a feeling. When building I try to project that feeling into the piece. I listen for that feeling in the piece as I build. Sometimes I hear different directions coming from the piece, and sometimes I follow those directions. It is not easy to communicate all of this or to experience it through another person. I am not sure if it is an entirely fair or possible thing to ask of another person.

But I am trying it. The alternative of giving up my clay work and pursuing a more cerebral and less physical form of art is one I acknowledge, but that I am not willing to choose right now. So I am working with an assistant to build the pieces for my next show.

Finding the right person to work with was important to me. When I first contemplated the thought, I realized how difficult it could be. The person would need to be familiar with clay-working techniques and also with the creative process. She or he, ideally, would be familiar with my work. Would ego be a problem? How would the work evolve?

It actually was not as difficult as I thought it would be to find someone, and, in retrospect, the choice was fairly obvious. I went to school at the University of Washington Ceramics Department with Janet Still in the 1980s. We became good friends and have kept track of each other's work. Janet's schedule and my finances limit us to working together one morning a week. She is patient and allows me to make decisions and change my mind, to be unsure. She is quiet and gives me time to think. Already there are issues of bonding. It perhaps is similar to surrogate motherhood. At some future point, it might be interesting to move toward collaboration—where both of us lend direction to a piece. This may be the way things evolve. For now, Janet is working at staying out of the way, of being my hands. It is a difficult but exciting process.

I return once again to God and the creative process. Perhaps the church continues the creative process that God started way back in the garden and redeemed through Jesus. We are God's hands now. Maybe God waits for us to assume our role as collaborators.

I will go on; we will go on. We will cry when we need to cry. I invite, I challenge us all to try always to keep our eyes and our ears and our hearts open to change and to the larger pattern of God at work in our lives and in our world.

Sandra Z. Richardson, Seattle, Washington, is an artist, who primarily uses clay as her medium.

Naming Sin and Communicating Compassion

by Ronald J. Sider

I recently preached a sermon at a Mennonite church presenting the biblical case for, among other things, caring for the poor, personal holiness, and marriage. Gently but clearly I held up the biblical standard of a loving, lifelong marriage covenant. The host pastor later suggested to me that my remarks were inappropriate for a congregation that included many Christians who had been divorced.

I find it difficult to name sin while effectively communicating love and compassion. There are several reasons for this difficulty. For starters, relativists chafe against any standards claiming to be universal. Many people confuse tolerance with relativism. Genuine tolerance means respecting others and defending their freedom of expression even when one believes that those views are wrong. But it does not mean throwing out the standards set forth in the Bible.

The heart that can say, *"Lord, I am sorry, I failed again. Please forgive me and change me so I stop doing what breaks your heart"* is very different from the one that says, *"There I go again upsetting the Puritans, but nobody's perfect so I don't need to feel guilty or try to change."*

The first position recognizes both biblical norms and divine mercy; the second does not.

A highly commendable desire to avoid being a "Christian Pharisee" can also lead to a one-sided emphasis. "Recovering Pharisees," an important article in the March/April issue of *Prism* magazine, reminded us to let the world know that Christians struggle and fail. Proud, self-righteous, "I'm-better-than-you-are" Christians are an abomination not just to their unbelieving neighbors, but also to God.

But is it not falling into the other extreme to say that "our sins . . . are no threat to our witness," or that showing the world our worst will "do more for the gospel than showing the world our best"?

Surely we can avoid Pharisaism without belittling sanctification.

So how can we name sin while communicating compassion?

First, let us remember that God has spoken, revealing right and wrong; therefore, these standards exist no matter what people feel or think.

Second, throughout the Bible we see God's prophets rebuking sin; today they would no doubt earn the label of "intolerant bigot" for some of their stances. St. Paul, nonetheless, bluntly says that adulterers, greedy persons, and lots of other sinners have "no inheritance in the kingdom of Christ" (Ephesians 5:5). He even urges excommunication from the Christian community (I Corinthians 5) for those who stubbornly refuse to repent. If God's biblical spokespersons clearly rebuked sin, faithful preachers and teachers today dare do no less.

Third, the New Testament clearly shows that God expects Christians to grow in grace. Walking with Christ, Christians undergo transformation. Grace, after all, refers not only to divine forgiveness but also to divine power that progressively makes us more Christlike. Part of the Good News is that Jesus' new messianic kingdom is becoming increasingly visible in the redeemed body of Christ.

Finally, Jesus—in his astounding, tender embrace of tax-collectors and prostitutes—is our perfect example. His parables demonstrate that God longs to forgive wandering prodicals. But while Jesus embraced sinners, he never overlooked sin, calling Peter Satan and denouncing the Pharisees as snakes and scorpions fit for hell (Matthew 23:23, 33). And they didn't like it!

Never forget that no matter how gentle and loving our words, when we clearly embrace God's word about sin, those who are unwilling to repent will resent it. This is why Jesus warned his followers that the world would hate them just as it hated him (John 7:7; 15:18-19).

Obviously, we must be very, very careful at this point. None of the above offers any excuse for spiritual pride, self-righteousness, lack of compassion, or failure to confess our ongoing struggles, mistakes—and yes, sins—as Christians.

My best advice for myself and others is to return repeatedly to Jesus' encounter with the woman caught in adultery (John 8:3-11). This broken woman could not doubt Jesus' love, acceptance, and forgiveness. The text overflows with Jesus' tender compassion, but his final word to her is clear: Please don't sin anymore. In Christ, compassion does not trump moral truth.

Ronald J. Sider, Philadelphia, Pennsylvania, is a prolific author and speaker, a professor of theology and culture, an editor, and president of Evangelicals for Social Action.

Embracing
the Struggle of Calling
by Ron Kraybill

"I want you to know how much I appreciate when you share personal experiences with us," said a student in class. Others around her nodded in agreement. In a spur-of-the-moment opening to class, I had just reflected for several minutes on my struggles in college and grad school to get work done, meet deadlines, and get papers in. In particular, I had recalled that I often wondered if I was smart or disciplined enough to do really well, whether I had what it took to excel in academia. Suddenly aware that I may be boring these undergrads with personal reflection about things that had nothing to do with the topic of the course, I had ended my reflections rather abruptly. Now to my surprise, one of them was asking for more, and it was clear from the faces of others that she spoke for many. "To me," she went on, "faculty look like they *always* knew what they were going to do, were good at what they do, and felt confident in the directions they took. It gives me hope for myself to realize that maybe you struggled, too, as a student."

The exchange has caused me to reflect on what happens between teachers and students. Several things stand out to me with great clarity. As a student I had many doubts about myself, my capacities to do serious work and meet the expectations of my professors, and my ability to "make the right decisions" in finding my calling. I had no idea that my teachers and professors might face similar self-doubts and struggles in regards to their own talents and callings. Although today I feel firmly emplanted in my calling, questions and self-doubt about what to do, and my ability to do what I am expected to do, remain an important part of my life. From conversations with friends and colleagues I know that I am not exceptional in this regard. The struggle to find our calling and confidence in our personal capacities is one that appears to follow most people throughout life.

It has taken me years to see that this struggle to be faithful to what God calls us to, and to have faith that our Creator has given us the gifts required to meet our calling, is not a weakness to be overcome. After all, fundamental questions of life are at stake: Who am I? What do I have to contribute to the world? How do I make my contribution?

For a person of faith, it is not a simple matter of answering such questions as lonely individuals. Others come into the equation: God, the community of faith, the larger human community. If we do not maintain an ongoing struggle with these questions throughout our lives, surely we are poor and unreflective stewards of the precious talents given to us. This means that the struggle to find and exercise joyous calling is a requirement of faithful stewardship of our lives. It is a painful gift that, openly received, teaches humility, attentiveness to God's ways of working in our lives, and openness to things we might otherwise ignore.

As a teacher, my highest hope is not to teach knowledge, but to help students learn to hear and respond to God's guidance through the ongoing quest for calling. A key ability I seek to cultivate is what Parker Palmer in *Let Your Life Speak* calls "listening to our lives." God speaks to us through our life experiences; particularly I believe, through the information provided by our dreams and passions. To get at this, I often ask students: If you could freely imagine yourself 10 years from now doing the things that you most long to do, the things that would bring you the deepest sense of joy and energy and life, what would you be doing? The initial reaction of most students makes it clear they have never been asked such a question before. They have been asked: What is your major? They have heard: What do you plan to do after graduation? But not: Towards what do your imagination and your heart, your wellsprings of joy and energy, point you?

After recovering from the shock of the question, most students have a great deal to say when given an opportunity to safely "dream" in the presence of a trusted mentor. Their responses often make "advising" easy. Whether the questions they face are about major concentrations of study, specific course selection, class projects or paper topics, the answers often come with surprising clarity when students are encouraged to listen to their imaginations and hearts. Of course, "reality" must enter the deliberations, too. But that is usually the easy part. Paying attention to God's guidance in our inner life is the unfamiliar part.

I have come to believe that if I want to teach students to seek and follow God's guidance regarding their lives, I must end the games of pretense I have often played about my own struggle for calling. I regret to admit that I have often allowed the world to press me into its mold of living a life of pretense about calling. How many times have I gone along with empty rituals of introductions that imply that credentials, publications, and years of experience make a person important, an all-knowing expert? How many times have I carefully shielded from my students and professional colleagues my own ongoing questions of competence and how to manage the unique package of strengths and weaknesses I represent? How often have I played the familiar game of projecting only strength, power, knowledge, and self-confidence to others, as though these are primary marks of a person faithful to calling? If my students are surprised to hear that someone like myself might have ongoing issues of struggle regarding calling, I have to recognize that I and others have given them an untrue picture of life, one that does not fit my own experience of calling.

Perhaps worse, my fear-driven participation in worldly pretenses of professional competence does not fit my values or my experience as a Christian who stands with a heart of constant questions before God. What do you want me to do, not only with my life, but with this year, this week, this day? Am I claiming the full capacities you have given me? Will you give me what I need to do that which I am called upon to do? What if I don't *feel* I have that? As I pursue my own response to call, do I recognize, celebrate, and call forth the abilities of others whom you have also created with unique gifts?

My convicted heart has driven me recently to seek opportunities to share with students these questions and the truth of my own struggle with calling. I have something to offer them in knowledge and skill in the topics of my courses. But there is something more important that I must not withhold, a full and honest reporting of my own experience with a struggle I believe every thoughtful student will live with throughout life.

Honesty begets honesty, and from the professor's choice to become vulnerable flows the possibility of meaningful individual relationships with students. As students come by to talk, I hope that they gain more than mere access to their professor. As I encourage students to examine and take seriously the call of their own hearts, to recognize and accept as a gift their own struggle to do well with the life God has given them, I hope to assist in the formation of a spiritual discipline that will last for a lifetime.

Ron Kraybill, Harrisonburg, Virginia, teaches in conflict studies and helps to direct the Institute of Peacebuilding at Eastern Mennonite University.

Pacifism—
And Women's Self-Defense

by Beth Graybill

What does it mean to do peace theological work experientially, in our bodies, as women and as Mennonites? Women survivors, and those who work around issues of rape prevention, sexual harassment, and battering, are familiar with women's responses to abuse or assault. Those of us from peace traditions bring an additional level of concern (or perhaps, guilt) to situations of potential or actual violence directed toward us as women. As Carol Penner has noted, Mennonite theology has traditionally not been helpful to victims of sexual abuse or assault. In fact, our tradition of nonresistance has often helped contribute to violence against women, by (implicitly) encouraging women to accept abuse as Christlike suffering. ("Mennonite Silences and Feminist Voices: Peace Theology and Violence Against Women," doctoral dissertation, unpublished.)

I approach the issue from several vantage points: as Women's Concerns director for Mennonite Central Committee (MCC), U.S., a position that puts me in touch with survivors of sexual abuse or assault in the wider Mennonite and Brethren in Christ churches; as an academic pursuing an advanced degree in Women's Studies; and as a rape survivor.

At the outset it seems important to say that a woman is never to blame for violence directed against her. Some of what passes for suggestions (nonviolent or otherwise) to women facing abuse overlooks the fact that the United States is a "rape-prone" society, as compared to countries like Japan, which are comparatively "rape-free" societies. We *should* live in a world where rape is unthinkable; the fact that it occurs is never a woman's fault, no matter what her response (or lack thereof).

Some pacifists may take the position that part of one's commitment to nonviolence is submitting to one's attacker as an example of loving one's enemies. I have respect for that position but I am not there. Violence against women, especially sexual abuse and assault, is a violation of bodily integrity that can have long-lasting consequences related to sexual intimacy and feeling unsafe in the world. I would never counsel someone to submit to that in the name of pacifism, whereas submitting in the face of overwhelming threat or force may be a rational choice that some women make in order to survive the rape.

I do think it was useful, as a woman, to have considered my response to the possibility of sexual assault before I had to face it. I am grateful to the Women's Studies literature I had read, most particularly a piece on "rape avoidance strategies." That article was based on interviews with several hundred women who'd been raped or assaulted. It documented that those women who had used one or more "avoidance strategies" were more likely to have avoided being raped. These strategies were not limited to fighting back but included such actions as screaming, trying to talk to or reason with one's attacker, non-cooperation (passive resistance), stalling for time (until help arrives), running away, etc.

I did all of those things. I also resisted my attacker by fighting for his knife. I don't know if I would have done that had he been armed with a gun. We were both cut. At one point I slid the knife under the refrigerator and fled while he retrieved his knife. He was later arrested and sentenced, based on DNA analysis of his blood left at the scene. Someone later commended me for responding nonviolently, although I'm not sure fighting back is in that category. In the moment, I did what I could to get away.

I was lucky. Not every woman is. And any woman is to be commended, not blamed, for whatever she did or didn't do to get through the attack. As a rape crisis counselor said to me some weeks after my assault, "I think it's great that you fought back, but that wasn't necessary. All that matters was that you survived the rape."

Part of my recovery after the assault was to take a self-defense course to rebuild my sense of physical safety in the face of violence directed against my person. And I also bought red-pepper spray. Some women buy big dogs. My rationale for the pepper spray was that it is temporary immobilizing but causes no permanent harm. I guess this is the principle of violence reduction that some in peace traditions espouse when complete nonviolence is impractical or impossible.

It is also important to note that when we think of pacifism and women's self-defense, we are usually assuming rape/assault by a stranger (my situation, which represents less than 15 percent of rape cases). By contrast, the far more common incidents of battering, sexual abuse, and assault are by persons known to the women. Nonviolent self-defense looks much different when we imagine the situation of date rape or pastoral sexual advances, let alone child abuse. I fear sometimes that laying nonviolent principles on women encourages our acceptance of these kinds of misogynist acts, rather than doing the hard work of confronting and getting such behavior stopped.

Moreover, when we speculate about violence and women, let's remember not to focus only on the easy stereotypes of stranger rape/assault with its often racist overtones. Let's instead help women confront the much more common and prevalent (based on my experience with survivors in MCC constituency churches) situations of sexual abuse and assault, including child molestation, among and within our churches.

Finally, relating nonviolently can occur after the rape, as well. Here, again, my situation was unique, in that my attacker was apprehended and received jail time; in general, even when a defendant is arrested for rape, the odds of sentencing him are small, though greater when the assailant is a man of color and the victim is white. I had opportunities during the legal proceedings to witness to my religious convictions. I, like most victims, was able to read a "Victim Impact Statement" in court, in which I admitted to feeling safer that he was no longer at large to victimize other women, but I was troubled by a legal system that viewed him as inhuman when I did not.

Probably most unusual, I also met with my rapist in a VORP (Victim-Offender Reconciliation Program) mediation after sentencing. He got to listen to my terror during the rape, and the aftermath of rebuilding trust and a sense of safety in the world. I got to understand how his own personal sense of being victimized led him to violate me, and possibly other women as well, and how hard it is to accept and take responsibility for one's own capacity for evil. Ultimately, his response made me mad, which was a great impetus to healing; you know, living well is the best revenge! That's probably not very pacifist, but it is therapeutic.

I wish that these reflections on my experience of surviving rape in the context of Mennonite peace theology could begin a long-overdue dialogue among Mennonite women about how the strands of peacemaking and violence against women inter-connect. I wish that it would become safe enough for those of us with such stories to overcome the difficulty in sharing them, for, by conservative estimates, one in four women nationwide has a story of violent assault or near-rape to tell.

Of course, our stories are hard to tell because being vulnerable can increase our sense of shame, which every survivor struggles with. And many of us have received misguided if not deliberately hurtful reactions that seem to blame us for having been so careless as to be raped. Quite honestly, it has been easier for me to write about my story, as Ruth Krall has noted in her dissertation research, since in some ways mine is a "success" story. Yet the healing for many of us is in coming to see ourselves as blameless for the experience, which, if we truly own this, can help us break from the silence.

Some years ago, while doing solidarity work on behalf of Guatemalan refugee women, I was struck with the poignancy of the weaving image. Guatemalan women weave, sitting on their heels, with a portable loom stretched in front of them, almost in an attitude of prayer. One end of the loom is tied to a tree, the other wrapped taut around their waist. Hands flashing, the woman moves her shuttle in and out, back and forth, weaving brilliantly colored, strong pieces of fabric.

This image is not limited to Latin America, since weaving—as well as quilting, needlepoint, knitting, and a variety of other sewing traditions—is women's work around the world. I have wondered what it would mean to think of a weaving mother God. How are the disparate and frayed threads of my own and other women's lives woven together into strands of strength and beauty?

The area of violence against women is seldom discussed in peace studies courses or contexts, but I believe it is time to bring those disparate threads together, since they connect in many women's lives.

As these threads begin to intertwine, so may the fabric of the Mennonite community's commitment to peacemaking include and invest in women's stories confronting violence.

Beth Graybill, Lancaster, Pennsylvania, is Women's Concerns director for Mennonite Central Committee.

By Hook or By Crook, We Kept Christmas

by Shirley Kurtz

Unfortunately, I got only the Christmas tree cookies baked and one long pan of chocolate-raspberry bars before, *whoosh*.

While the cookies—beaten butter, egg yolks, flour, powdered sugar, rolled out and cut into fancy shapes—were still hot from the oven, I'd poked the holes for the strings. Some of the cookies crumbled, and more than just the ruined ones got devoured, but plenty were left to hang on the tree. Up close, it smelled faintly sweet.

I'd not let the boys and Paulson, my husband, sample the chocolate-raspberry bars. "Not yet," I said when they wheedled. "Aw, c'mon," protested Christopher and Zachary, but I stuck the entire panful in the freezer to take to the relatives in Pennsylvania on Christmas day. I'd started with a chocolate cake batter, adding dollops of sweetened cream cheese and a cup of chocolate chips, and after this baked I'd layered on top a raspberry sauce spread thinly, and melted dark chocolate drizzled in crisscross lines. Um, um.

I'd planned to make pies yet, rich crusted and full of pecan chunks in thick goo. Also cinnamon-orange buns; nobody was supposed to eat the single orange

I'd bought and stowed in the refrigerator. I would slather the flattened dough with butter, brown sugar, cinnamon, and orange-rind snippets, and roll it up. After the buns came out of the oven I would ice them with a runny orange-rind glaze. The aroma would be heavenly.

Or so I thought. But December 14, Saturday lunchtime, with everybody's cheese sandwiches toasting in the skillet on the stove, the oven knob suddenly ignited and flames whooshed a foot high. I'd *thought* I smelled leaking gas. At least I wasn't hovering right then, flipping the sandwiches. But so much for my oven gone kaput. It would be several weeks till the part needed for repair could be obtained. On the phone with our newlywed daughter living in Virginia, I bewailed my plight. "Poor you," Jennifer clucked sympathetically. This close to Christmas, I would have to do some finagling to maintain our usual level of holiday revelry and keep our senses and cravings sated.

Sunday afternoon I badgered Christopher about inviting his friends over. Bethany and Kristin at church had told him about their plans to bake cookies. "Say they have to bring cookies," I urged, "if they want to come." After he telephoned, I dashed around straightening up the house. Goodness, I hadn't put up the nativity scene yet. Hastily unpacking our wooden set, I arranged the tiny carved pieces on the windowsill above the kitchen sink. I sticky-tacked the angel to the windowpane, positioned above the baby. I placed a red candle near the baby, too. It flickered and cast a holy-ish glow, and now we *looked* ready for Chistmas, anyway. And wonder of wonders, when the girls arrived they were bearing not frankincense and myrrh but a big Tupperware container full of spicy gingerbread people decorated to look like our family, including Jennifer's husband. There was also a plateful of other gingerbread cut-outs, some thickly frosted. We eagerly consumed every last crumb. Since John and Jennifer weren't here we could gobble their "people," too.

By hook or by crook we would manage to keep Christmas. And my birthday as well, which falls close and always adds to the merrymaking. During the week, while I was gone, Christopher mixed up a cake with coconut in it and whipped egg whites. He carried the batter in layer pans down the road to the neighbors' to bake in their oven. I was flabbergasted when I learned of this. We feasted on the cake, and then a few days later we stocked up on donuts, boxfuls from the grocery store: glazed, sugared cake, apple fritter, plus an assortment of especially gross jelly- and pudding-filled. We were planning to Christmas carol that night with Yoders and Brennemans, go around trumpeting the news of the Child born to deliver us from our sins, and had promised to feed everyone afterwards at our house. So at least, now we were back to celebrating *Jesus'* birthday. Well, so to speak. Gathered around the table with our friends, we crammed our bellies. Zachary ate himself sick.

Only a few donuts remained, the day before Christmas. The boys worried that these wouldn't be enough to hold us over till we got to Pennsylvania. In the afternoon at Wal-Mart (this is getting really embarrassing), the woman's voice blaring over the loudspeaker announced a donut special in the bakery, one dozen for $1.87. Zachary pushing our cart grabbed pleadingly at my arm. "No!" I snapped. And then, "Oh, well. Sure. I don't care." He and Paulson hurried off to pick up our dozen.

We went to bed stuffed, again. Christmas morning I laid bags of candy beside everyone's plates at the breakfast table. Christmas evening in Pennsylvania at the Bainbridge relatives' we gorged on raisin-filled cookies, chocolate chip, sugar, thumbprint, lemon squares, cartwheels, snickerdoodles, *Mennonite Community Cookbook* date pinwheels, *More with Less* molasses crinkles. Everybody declared if I entered my chocolate-raspberry bars in the Pillsbury Bake-Off I'd win the $25,000 prize. The next morning at Grandma's we oohed over her iced apricot-cherry bread. Lunchtime at Millers' there was cranberry-cherry pie. At Stoltzfuses' in the evening, chocolate-frosted chocolate cake with globs of whipped topping and cherries. We drove back home to West Virginia with my pan of chocolate-raspberry bars only half emptied. I plunked it back in the freezer.

Eight precious pieces were still uneaten when John and Jennifer arrived New Year's Eve. "What shall we bring?" Jennifer had asked on the phone the day before, knowing I still couldn't bake, and now they were merrily hauling in breads, cookies, pecan squares as rich and sweet as any pie, and two cakes. We staggered around the house that night and next day. "Your chocolate-raspberry bars aren't all gone?" Jennifer exclaimed. "Oh, goody. Let's have those, too."

January 2 or 3 I pulled the butter cookies off the brittle Christmas tree. Soon after, I took the little wooden nativity pieces one by one from the kitchen windowsill, brushed off the dust, and rewrapped them in their scraps of tissue paper. The lambs. Cows. Gaunt shepherds. The wise men, rather sober. The brooding angel. (When I tugged it loose from the windowpane it fell into the sink and got a bit damp.) Joseph looked bemused, I thought, and Mary weary and swollen. Not from overeating. Last of all I tucked away the little Lord Jesus, carved oddly out of proportion, it seemed to me, the body too small for its head and old-person face.

Jesus' expression seemed careworn, almost pained, as if he was grieving. But perhaps I was just imagining things.

Shirley Kurtz is a writer who lives in Keyser, West Virginia.

Shaken Security

by James M. Sensenig

The unprecedented terrorist attack in the United States has shaken the security of this nation and the world. In the past, United States citizens have been relatively secure compared to many people in the world. We have not seen war and destruction as many other nations have. The recent events have shaken that security in a way this generation has not known before.

Events like this do affect us. Our hearts go out in sympathy to those who have been touched directly by the deaths. We also are touched by the many who are suffering physically. It also makes us wonder what the future will hold. It causes us to reflect and to take a fresh hold on that which endures.

These events should cause us to evaluate where our security lies. Do we trust in earthly kingdoms, or do we trust in the Lord? Our response does say something about our trust. "Some trust in chariots, and some in horses: but we will remember the name of the Lord our God" (Psalm 20:7).

Times like these should move us to prayer. The government and all in authority should be a part of our daily prayers. We must rest in God, the sovereign one, who can turn the heart of the king whithersoever He will (Proverbs 21:1). We should thank the Lord for the freedom and protection we have enjoyed in the past.

We should not become caught up in the emotional frenzy that accompanies events like this. Jesus said when we hear of wars and rumors of wars we should not be troubled. The Scriptural advice for us is to watch and be sober.

Events like this remind us that we live in the end time. We certainly see an increase of violence, which is prophesied in the Scriptures. Jesus said when we see "distress of nations, with perplexity" and "men's hearts failing them for fear," we should "then look up . . . for [our] redemption draweth nigh" (Luke 21:25-28). The end of time is nearing.

We may need to face more suffering as we approach the end time. This should not cause us to fear, but it should drive us closer to the Lord. God's people sometimes have to suffer with the wicked. Those who have the hope of heaven should be the best able to face whatever the Lord allows into their lives.

The hardships we may face could bring greater opportunities to proclaim the Gospel. Paul rejoiced when circumstances presented additional opportunity to preach the Gospel even though it meant more suffering for him (Philippians 1:12-18). Christ is the one who can be the anchor to our soul when security is shaken around us.

We must continue to keep ourselves fortified in our nonresistant stand. We could very quickly be confronted with a situation of military conscription. We must not get caught up in the war spirit and hatred that is so apparent. It is a good opportunity for us to display the love of God by our attitudes and actions.

We must remember we are not a part of this world's system. Even though we are citizens of this nation, our primary citizenship is in heaven. Jesus said, "My kingdom is not of this world: if my kingdom were of this world, then would my servants fight" (John 18:36).

We must always keep in mind that we make our greatest contribution to the country by being a salt to the earth and a light to the world. We can faithfully fill that role as we live in faithful obedience to the Scriptures. The events should be a call to greater Christian commitment. We must "be diligent that [we] may be found of him in peace without spot, and blameless" (2 Peter 3:14).

James Sensenig, Johnsonville, Illinois, is an ordained minister in the Eastern Pennsylvania Mennonite Church and editor of The Eastern Mennonite Testimony.

To the Mennonite Churches of the United States of America: *A Message of Gratitude, Condolence, and Hope*

by Ricardo Esquivia Ballestas

Brothers and Sisters, may the peace of Jesus Christ guide you, accompany you, and comfort you.

Confronted with the terrible happenings in New York and Washington September the 11th, I have two strong feelings on my heart as I write to you. One is of gratitude and the other is of condolence, and the two meet to produce a great yearning for faith and hope.

My feeling of gratitude arises in response to acts of tremendous love and solidarity that you have shown for the situation of pain, destruction, death, and hopelessness that we, the people of Colombia, have suffered as a result of injustice, cruelty, and terrorism practiced by the armed groups, legal and illegal, in our territory.

I see the face of God in your faces, my beloved brothers and sisters, in the acts of solidarity that are manifestations of tenderness among people. I saw how these small seeds of hope and love are growing between our peoples. I saw that among us, the global

49

family of faith, the universe is our homeland and in this way we are not strangers, but sisters and brothers in faith, in love, and in hope.

I send my condolences, accompanied by fraternal pain, which arise in response to the images of destruction and death and the dazed and incredulous faces seen on television during the terrorist attack suffered by your nation, the most powerful in the world today.

I think that this act brings us closer together. Now that you, too, have experienced pain and fear, it's not necessary for you to imagine what it's like to live with insecurity and to be exposed to a terrorist attack. Now that you have lived through it, you know that no government, no matter how strong, can protect us from the effects of evil, injustice, hate, and revenge.

With troubled hearts and tears in our eyes we say to you, may God protect you brothers and sisters. We understand, feel, and share your pain because it is also ours. We are one in the body of Christ and "when one part of the body suffers, the whole body suffers." We know what it means to suffer, the pain and the lashing of injustice, because this has been our daily bread all our lives. Who better than we to understand you, sisters and brothers, than we who have learned through our own misfortune? For this reason we tell you with deep pain in our souls that we understand your pain. May God comfort you and give you strength and courage to transform these acts for good, and not be tempted by seductive feelings of hatred and revenge.

While it is important that acts that destroy human life not end in impunity, Romans 12:17-21 invites us not to take revenge into our own hands, but to allow

God to bring justice. We are called to overcome evil with good.

Now for my yearning for faith and hope. It is not new but rather makes itself manifest at this time. It has always been present, and my gratitude, combined with my condolences, only serve to make it more visible and necessary in these critical moments.

Through the apostle Paul we know that in these end times, faced with violence and injustice, creation is crying out with birthing pain, and we, the global family of faith, groan with it, waiting for redemption. Brothers and sisters, every birth is painful. Through these acts that we suffer, God is trying us and inviting us to be birth parents of the new history where evil is overcome by good, where the enemy is loved, where we can all live without fear, and where nations respect the human dignity of all people on earth.

The solidarity that you have always shown for the pain of other peoples must not be lost with these recent acts that affect you directly. Rather, may your compassion increase with your own suffering and permit you to understand that it is in your country that the birthing process must begin. At this time the United States is the center of the world, and what is done there has positive and negative repercussions in the other countries of the world. Citizens of the United States, like all other peoples, will enjoy or suffer the consequences sooner or later. "He who sows righteousness reaps a sure reward" (Proverbs 11:18).

It seems very symbolic that precisely this passage on birthing new life (Romans 8:22-23) is included in Paul's letter to the Romans, given that Rome was the center of the world in those times. I believe that this is a direct message to all the church of Christ that finds itself in the center of world political power, and that is where you are. What a great challenge and responsibility has come upon you today!

For this reason, brothers and sisters, having known your solidarity, your commitment to the message of Jesus, having been witnesses to your generosity, having known your capacity for biblical interpretation and above all your great human feeling, the global family of faith looks to you, filled with hope that you, from the center of the world, will begin a great campaign to keep the effects of evil, of hate, and of revenge from nesting in the souls of leaders and governments of the countries of the West. May you impede them from using their economic and military might against the people of the East and of the Third World who are as innocent as the inhabitants of New York and Washington, who were victims of humans alienated by pain, hate, and hunger for vengeance.

Let us unite in a great campaign of fasting, prayer, preaching, and song, and in so doing rise to the challenge of taking to your leaders, the government of the United States, and the governments to the West and to the East, the message that violence only brings more violence, that "hate is like salt water; the more one drinks, the thirstier one gets." It is time for the peoples of the earth to treat one another with respect, dignity, and solidarity. Only then can they calm the thirst of hate and vengeance felt by people who have historically been mistreated. War will only produce more hate and vengeance, and the people of the United States will not have peace and will only live in permanent anxiety.

To the Mennonite Churches of the United States of America

It is time to birth a new world order, and the people of the United States have the historic opportunity to show the rest of the world how to really live civilly and with justice, without violence, without acts of death and destruction of innocent human lives, to return evil with good and to take away from the terrorists the excuse for a holy war of hate and death.
With appreciation, respect, and gratitude,
Your brother in Christ and humanity,
Ricardo Esquivia Ballestas

Ballestas is a member of the Mennonite church in Colombia, Director of the Commission of Human Rights and Peace of the Council of Evangelical Churches in Columbia (CEDECOL), and Director of Justapaz.

God's Spirit
and a Theology for Living
by David Kline

The most commonly used prayer book in Amish
homes is *Die Ernsthafte Christenpflicht* (The Serious
Christian Duty). It dates to the early 1700s and the
Palatinate Mennonites and also was common in many
Mennonite homes, especially Swiss/German, until the
Great Awakening of the late 1800s. Among prayers for
many occasions, the small volume contains several
evening (*Abend*) prayers.

I have a small, slightly condensed edition of the
Christenpflicht. It was printed during 1826 in Wooster,
Ohio, by Johann Sala. My parents got it when my
grandparents' estate was divided among the heirs
back in the early 1950s. On page 10 is the evening
prayer *"Ein schön Abend-Gebet täglich zusprechen,"*
translated as "A nice evening-prayer to be read daily."
The lower outside edges of those pages are so thumb-
worn that the print is hard to read; the pages were
illuminated countless times by the light of a candle or
kerosene lamp.

Toward the end of the five-page prayer is the line
*"und lasz uns deine Creaturen and Geschöpf nicht verder-
ben sondern dasz wir sur ewigen Seligkeit mögen gebracht
und erhalten werden."* Literally, this translates as "and
help us not to harm your creatures and creation but

that we may be brought to eternal salvation and may abide therein." I like a friend's translation: "and help us be gentle with your creatures and handiwork so that we may abide in your eternal salvation and continue to be held in the hollow of your hand." There, I think, lies the Anabaptist theology for living. Maybe, as I recently read somewhere, a man travels the world over in search of what he needs and returns home to find it. That line of the evening prayer swirls in a wispy cloud of controversy, of course. Good Anabaptists would not pray such an earth-centered prayer, would they? After all, our salvation does not hinge on how we care for creation or on what we claim as our profession.

To confuse the issue further, later editions of the *Christenpflict* have commas inserted *"und lasz uns deine Creaturen und Geschöpf nicht verderben,"* which shifts the focus of the prayer to us humans as God's creatures and handiwork and away from the rest of God's creation. Maybe our local Wooster printer Johann plucked out the commas on his own initiative. The point is that hundreds of fathers and mothers belonging to the Anabaptist branch of Christendom did pray and believe exactly as the line of prayer reads in the Wooster edition of the prayer book.

A Theology of Living for Today's Anabaptists

Why is it that some of today's Anabaptists are having such a difficult time finding a theology for living? Could it be that we have become too alienated from the land to which our foreparents felt so closely connected and simply can no longer relate to the creation? Creation has become something distant, something you go to, but has ceased to be a living part of us. Are we merely residing on the land instead of living with it? If we would believe that line of prayer without the commas, we would take care of God's creation because our lives depend on it. We would believe that "the earth is the Lord's and the fullness thereof."

We are friends of a young family whose farm was threatened by a housing development. The houses would have shattered the sanctity and privacy of their farm. When my friend told me what might happen, he had tears in his eyes. "I will weep if I leave, and I will weep if I stay. But I have to stay; the farm has been too good to us. I can't turn my back to these fields and pastures and trees [we were looking across his 80-acre farm] that have nurtured and shaded our animals. In turn the animals have nurtured us, which has given us a good life." That young family needs no theology for living; they are living it. (Fortunately the housing plans fell through.)

The Mennonites and Amish have a long history of being stewards of the land. When the Palatinate Mennonite David Mellinger was asked in the 1700s about his success as a clover farmer, he replied, "I should have already given princes and other great lords a description of my operation and how I achieved it but I cannot tell it so easily. One thing leads to another. It is like a clockwork where one wheel grabs hold of another and then the work continues without my even being able to know or describe how I brought the machine into gear."[1] Louis Bromfield, novelist and later an innovative farmer on Malabar Farm near Mansfield, Ohio, wrote in his delightful book *Pleasant Valley* (1940) that the Amish and Mennonites are the only farmers in America who have stayed on the land they settled and have kept improving it.

Sadly, many Anabaptist families proved that "a man standing in his own field is unable to see it," as Emerson is thought to have said. They looked longingly at the industrial society and, to use an Amish phrase, jumped the fence from an agrarian life to an industrial one. Here is when the tendency to become an exploiter instead of a nurturer had its beginnings. When that link to the land or the earth is severed, life revolves around plastic, asphalt, steel on rubber, false-security lights—human-created things—and the weather becomes something to complain about or escape from. The beauty of the changing seasons is of minor significance. Nature becomes an adversary, something to be subdued and altered to one's liking, a resource from which to profit, seldom loved for its own sake.

Early Anabaptists looked at the earth not as an adversary but as a friend. Even bad weather had its advantages. When the weather was too miserable for the *Taeufer Jaeger* (Anabaptist hunters) to venture out, the believers had an opportunity to assemble for worship. Caves and forests sheltered them for secret meetings. The Jura Mountains became a sanctuary for those fleeing persecution in the Emmenthal. Perhaps that reliance on nature's protection is one of the reasons Anabaptists never much cared for purging from their everyday lives what today would be considered pagan practices. When pagan Europe was Christianized, great efforts were made to eradicate every practice of pagan or earth worship to create a distinct division between Christian and pagan practices. Since Anabaptist forebears were so rural and closely tied to the land that gave them sustenance, some "earthy" practices survived in their lives and rituals.[2]

The Anabaptist register of Scriptures (all New Testament) and hymns (from the *Ausbund*) tends to be seasonal, especially the hymns. In the spring we sing of the skylark trilling its love song and in the autumn of the coming cold season. Farm families prefer an autumn wedding because much of the food for the wedding dinner can be raised or grown during spring and summer—the corn and potatoes; stock for the dressing; apples for the pies; strawberries for jam; lettuce, broccoli, and cauliflower for salads; and broilers for fried chicken. The Old Order Amish still have their weddings on Thursdays and sometimes Tuesdays. (The more liberal Amish have switched from Thursday to Saturday, echoing the trend from agrarian to industrial.)

According to William Schreiber, "The Amish have preserved for modern society the clear traces of ancient pagan culture which pre-date the Christian era; cults based upon the worship of the pre-Christian Germanic gods Ziu and Donar (*Donnerstag—* Thursday). In this more than in any other phase of their distinctive life, the Amish form a cultural enclave stronger and more cohesive than any other known within modern America." Thursday is still the preferred day for weddings in parts of southern Germany. In rural South Germany one still heard in 1962, *Donnerstagheirat–Glücksheirat* (Thursday wedding–lucky wedding). "Here [South Germany] the god Donar was the preeminently revered god of marriage and of course it must be added that he is the god of agriculture, of the livestock, and of fertile growth. Practically all farm life and increase was his special domain."[3]

Ascension Day, which always comes on a Thursday, is observed by the Amish as a day of fasting and prayer, a holy day. Interestingly, the nation of Germany observes Ascension Day in the same manner. Stores are closed and no trucks are allowed to travel on that day. The early Anabaptists (and now the Amish) were an earth-bound people who showed a reverence for creation and the earth. They never felt the angst of modern Christianity's separation from nature. As our young son once asked, "If Heaven is such a beautiful place and the earth is so bad, why are people so reluctant to let go of life?"

Some scholars claim that the hymns sung by the Amish in church are simply the melodies of rural folk songs from the sixteenth century adapted to the *Ausbund* hymnal. Many of these hymns were written by believers in prison. Musicologists think that the hymns are also connected to Gregorian chants.

And I would guess that more Amish than will admit to it still plant some of their seeds according to certain astrological signs. My father would sow the spring clover in the sign of Leo in March. Some neighbors plant their potatoes on or the day after the May full moon, radishes in a waning moon, and above-ground crops in a waxing moon. Fence posts were dug in during a waning moon to prevent heaving and to ensure that there would be enough soil to tamp in and fill around the post. Dousing, or water "witching," is still a fairly common practice in spite of accusations of witchcraft. *Brauching*, which somewhat crudely translates as powwowing, used to be commonly practiced by a small number of healers in the community.

As a child I developed a severe case of hives. Late one evening my parents took me to a local *Braucher*, who moved his hands over the affected parts of my anatomy, all the while saying something I could not understand. What I did understand was that the next morning my miserable hives were gone. A story is told about how Dr. Hostetler came down with erysipelas, a condition his own medications could not cure. One night, like Nicodemus to Jesus, Dr. Hostetler walked the mile across the fields to Brauch Jake, who cured him with one treatment. No one argues with success. Why, as a friend asked recently, would an evil spirit want to heal? I have struggled not too successfully for a long time with Western culture's world-view that alienates itself from nature. The earth is perceived as only a stage on which to work out our destinies, and the creation—trees, plants, insects, mammals, even the constellations—as merely props in the drama. We say that nature exists solely for our benefit, a vast supply warehouse to let us live sumptuously without regard for tomorrow.

Another point that has me puzzled is why some Christians argue so vehemently against the theory of evolution and then abuse the God-created earth as if they have a God-given right to do so? They seem not to have any qualms about being part of the systematic destruction of the natural world for the sake of human greed. There is much to be lost by such arrogance and lack of reverence for creation and its Creator. Recently, I was given a summarized copy of

Dr. W. C. Lowdermilk's 1939 timeless report on the historic loss of 27 of the world's civilizations. Civilizations and their great cities collapsed because the land that nurtured them was abused and depleted to the point of infertility. Babylon became, as the Hebrew prophets had warned, "a desolation, a dry land . . . and wolves shall cry in their castles."[4] Ironically, when Dr. Lowdermilk visited Babylon in the late 1930s, the only living thing he saw in the desolated city was a lean and rangy wolf. He viewed the ruins of Carthage and Timgad and the north coast of Africa, at one time the "granary of Rome," its hillsides bare of topsoil, even though the valley floors are still cultivated. Many of the ancient cities are buried by soil eroded from surrounding slopes, soil that at one time had made the cities prosperous. Out of Dr. Lowdermilk's shocking report on the devastation early civilizations suffered from lack of land stewardship, the U.S. Soil Conservation Service was born—a novel attempt to reverse the direction in which our nation was heading.

We say we know better now. We have learned from history. We have better technology with which to combat the forces that ravage the land. But do we? To save the soil we rely on disturbing amounts of chemicals and pesticides. Recently, I helped identify and then draw blood samples from Amish people with Parkinson's disease in a study conducted by Ohio State University working jointly with the University of Miami (Florida) under a grant from the federal government. Interestingly, Miami, New Orleans, and Millersburg, Ohio, have what researches call *clusters* of Parkinson's sufferers, levels much

higher than in the rest of the nation. The theoretical
cause in Ohio is pesticides. Almost all Ohio patients
are men and were active farmers in the early 1950s,
when the insecticide heptachlor, a chlorinated hydrocarbon closely related to DDT, was heavily used to
control spittlebugs in hay fields. The experts advised
farmers to use this new technology because it was
effective and long-lasting. According to a professor
and researcher at the Ohio Research and
Development Center, even after 40 years, chlorinated
hydrocarbon residues are still in the soil and, when
the conditions are right, the persistent chemical
volatilizes out of the soil and is reabsorbed by the
crops.

How does a person or a church go about finding a
theology for living? An Amish bishop from
Pennsylvania said, "We should conduct our lives as if
Jesus would return today but take care of the land as
if He would not be coming for a thousand years."
The "eleventh commandment," which Dr.
Lowdermilk gave in a talk on stewardship in
Jerusalem in 1939, is interesting: Thou shalt inherit
the holy earth as a faithful steward, conserving its
resources and productivity from generation to generation. "Thou shalt safeguard thy fields from soil erosion, thy living waters from drying up, thy forests
from desolation and protect thy hills from overgraz-
ing by thy herds, that thy descendants may have
abundance forever. If any shall fail in this stewardship of the land thy fruitful fields shall become ster-
ile stony grounds and wasting gullies, and thy
descendants shall decrease and live in poverty or
perish from the face of the earth."[5]

One Man's Way of Caring for Creation

My father practiced what Dr. Lowdermilk preached. My parents married in 1929 and began working a "farmed out" property sold at a sheriff's sale. In his 40 years of farming, my father did what Bernd Längin wrote that the Amish strive to do: "Land ought to be treated and developed so that parents can face future generations without shame for what they have done to the earth."[6] When he handed the operation of the farm over to my wife and me in 1968, my father had to feel no shame; it had been cared for lovingly. "When you send forth your spirit, they are created; and you renew the face of the earth" (Psalm 104:30 NRSV).

Father died in March 1993. That first spring and summer, I was unable to return to his grave, for reasons I can't really explain. In September I walked the mile across the fields and woods to my brother's farm, where Dad is buried. On the way over I picked up a red tail feather lost by a molting hawk, a feather that had soared high over our farm but now, too, had fallen to earth. Entering the small *Friedhof*, I knelt and "planted" the feather on the mound of fresh soil on Dad's grave. Then I rose and looked over the neighborhood where the red-tailed hawk hunted voles, screamed its shrill cry from high in the cloudless sky, and raised its young—a land of fields and woods loved by the hawk and its mate and loved, too, by my father.

Looking down into the valley of Salt Creek, I recalled the many times Dad and I had walked along its meandering course through the pastures. Sometimes fishing, sometimes mushrooming, sometimes returning from a coon hunt, the walk was always pleasurable. Then I raised my eyes and looked at the farmsteads. To the east and south there hardly was a set of buildings that my father did not have a hand in building. Many of the barns had timbers he had sawn on his little sawmill. He never missed a barn raising or work "frolic" in the neighborhood. He enjoyed the camaraderie, he loved to help, and his skills in carpentry were useful.

Dad gave more to the world and its inhabitants than he took. He became native to this place, living on and from the land. Toward the end of his life, he told me, "Eighty-seven. It sounds like a long time. But it wasn't; it was a short time."

I think it was so because he loved life—the creation and the joys of seeing and being a part of it all. He never saw the Pacific or the redwoods or the Grand Canyon or even the Mississippi, and I don't think he felt deprived for not having beheld those natural wonders because he "saw" so much around home. He could tell every kind of tree by looking at its bark at eye level. He knew the locations of the only persimmon and cucumber trees in the area. Likewise, Dad knew every raccoon den tree for miles around. He would show me where the coons would climb a smaller tree that leaned to the limbs of the larger den tree—he could tell by the claw scratches on the bark. He never knowingly cut down a tree that was home to a raccoon or squirrel. When a neighbor sold an old sugar maple that was a den tree, Dad found it almost sacrilegious. Of course, he didn't tell the neighbor his feelings. When working in the fields, Dad could tell at a glance whether a large, soaring bird was a red-tailed hawk (long broad wings and fanned tail) or a turkey vulture (longer and narrower wings held in a slight dihedral). He knew the slower, ganglier wingbeats of the northern harrier (marsh hawk, he called it) and the swift wingbeats of the speedy Cooper's hawk. He could tell the condition of the soil by studying the "weed" plants growing in the field. If sorrel (sour vines in the dialect) grew, he knew the field needed lime. Pesky quack grass indicated a calcium deficiency.

Dad absolutely abhorred fall plowing. Leaving the freshly plowed, bare soil exposed over winter to wind and water erosion was totally unthinkable. It was much harder on the field than taking off a crop, he insisted. My guess is that his aversion went deeper than concern over soil erosion—plowing in autumn's chill just doesn't sit right. Plowing should be done in the renewal of spring when one shucks off the coat of winter and rolls up shirt sleeves to the returning sun and Gulf-warmed wind, which bring with them the meadowlarks and pipits and vesper sparrows, ideal plowing companions. I can easily see why ancient cultures in northern climates worshipped the sun. We farmers in the spring almost do.

My father's thinking on caring for creation was influenced by a Mennonite schoolteacher he had from second through eighth grades, Clarence F. Zuercher. Forty years later Mr. Zuercher became my teacher in the second grade and taught me for seven years. Both Mr. Zuercher and my father were descended from Swiss immigrants, and both were farmers and loved the outdoors. I will not get into the creation-caring methods Mr. Zuercher used for teaching, but he never let the classroom interfere with his students' education. If one's livelihood comes from the earth—from the land, from creation on a sensible scale, where humans are a part of the unfolding of the seasons, experience the blessings of drought-ending rains, and see God's spirit in all creation—a theology for living should be as natural as the rainbow following a summer storm. And then we can pray, *"Und lasz uns deine Creaturen und Geschöpf nicht verderben"* (And help us to walk gently on the earth and to love and nurture your creation and handiwork).

I Mellinger, cited in Correll, Ernst H. *Dar schweizerische Taeufermennonitentum,* Tuebingen: J.C.B. Mohr (Paul Siebak), 1925, 125-126.

2 Schreiber, William. *Our Amish Neighbors,* Chicago: University of Chicago Press, 1962.

3 Ibid., 186-187, 188.

4 Lowdermilk, C.W. *Conquest of the Land through Seven Thousand Years.* Bulletin 99. Washington, D.C.: U.S. Department of Agriculture, 1948, 4.

5 Ibid., 30.

6 Längin, Bernd. *Plain and Amish,* Scottdale, PA: Herald Press, 1994, 56.

David Kline is a farmer and writer from Fredericksburg, Ohio.

Short Fiction, I

The Kiss
March, 1810
by Evelyn Miller

I did not want the Kiss. For six months I have lived
with this Kiss on my cheek; I still do not want it. I am
ashamed to say that I am one of the Lord's anointed
and I would rather spurn the call. Sarah says I looked
unsteady when Bishop Blauch called my name and
gave me his right hand to stand. Our beloved patri-
arch has tottered for years. Perhaps unsteadiness
comes with the task.

To be a farmer. That is all I ever cared about. To till
the land and tend the sheep. Now I have been given
these critters that walk upright and carry stubborn
hearts. I do not know how to keep them in line. But
here I am, Isaac Joder, a Minister of the Book. Sarah
says that sometimes we are given what we do not
seek; when the call comes, we must answer. Sarah
reminds me it is a Holy Kiss. Then she kisses me on
the lips and flickers her eyebrows.

Another thing I do not want: this roundness about
the waist. It makes me look shorter and shorter as I
take on this wide girth. Sarah smiles and says there is
that much more goodness to spread; then she passes
me another cake. I eat because the buckwheat has
lasted well. I eat before it gets wormy.

None of that matters. Worse by far than the round-

ness, I do not know how to mend this rift between
brothers. I fear it will end in shunning, and I shrink
from that as I would from knocking an active hornet's
nest to the ground. Someone else has disturbed the
nest and I stand in the midst, surrounded by an angry
swarm.

Last October the ordained brethren from all over—
Berks and Mifflin, Chester, Lancaster, as well as our
own county—agreed that there must be more unifor-
mity. Shunning those who err. Placing under the ban
those who commit grievous deeds. I agreed with the
counsel of the brethren. But I have no desire to drink
this cup. I want to wash my hands of the enforcement. Sarah could apply it, but of course, she is a
woman. Bishop Blauch imparts wisdom from his store
of years, but we cannot expect him to come all the
way from the Brothers Valley whenever a controversy
takes place among rival parties. With eleven families
in our River district we easily have need of our own
minister. But I did not seek it.

Sarah says I am more of a stay-at-home, unlike my
father and brothers. It is something of a distinction to
say that the Samuel Joder who is the first white settler in Ohio is my father. At one time I had thought to
follow. Part of me wanted to go; part of me held back.
Now I have one foot nailed to the ground. Perhaps the
Kiss is for the good; I do not believe I could subject
Sarah and my little ones to such unknowns.

Father showed me the deeds for their first exploring party, signed by Mr. Thomas Jefferson. That was
almost three years ago, when Father and some others
thought to establish an Amish colony farther west.
They traveled all that summer through wilderness,

from Pittsburgh down the Ohio River, through more forest, up north again on the Mississippi. Several locations appeared inviting for settlement, but they made no commitment. When they returned by land on the northern route, they ended in that place called Ohio and liked well what they saw.

Only a year later, my father and brothers had made up their minds and headed back to make their stay in Ohio. The next spring Father returned to fetch Mother and the younger ones and all their belongings. He said nothing of the privations of winter. I know things could not have been easy. He went on at length about huge forests full of oak, springs everywhere, hills that lacked the steepness we have here. He did not tell it all. I know that. If I had not received this call to minister to the flock along the Casselman, I might be out the door, following his glowing report. The Kiss has kept me from that danger. I fear that Father neglects his own call to the Book because of this lure of new land. I have never heard of a faithful Shepherd of those who Wander.

At the age of eighteen. That is when my first call came. "Isaac, where is my servant?" It came at night as I slept. I answered and joined the church. How easy then to promise to do whatever the church called me to. Had someone ventured that the Kiss would land on my cheek, I would have laughed. That was for other men and old ones.

Then the call came again. Later and louder. I was shearing sheep. "Isaac, I am the Lord Thy God. Hearken to my voice." I covered my ears but I could not quench the summons. On that Sunday morning those of us named as candidates were called forward to sit opposite Brother Blauch. I sat with my hands in front of me, my fingers interlocked. I was not accustomed to attention such as this. To be a farmer. That is all I want. Even then, sitting at the front, I had no notion. How could it fully register? The changes to come. I have wondered since if our Lord knew that Judas was going to kiss him before it happened. Perhaps he too was caught looking the other way. Knowing only in part.

I was as one struck dumb. Words were said. Stories told from Scripture. Sarah reminds me that young Timothy was admonished by the apostles when he was chosen. In the same way, I was instructed with regard to the teaching, preaching, and praying that I must do. I was to begin at once. That was a shock. I walked in a farmer; I walked out a preacher. Sealed by a Kiss. I was told that I would continue as long as I was found blameless. I went to church that day a normal man; I left with a mantle I did not seek.

For nights I slept little. I pined for my father and brothers in their new spot they call Sugarcreek. I could have escaped with that adventure. Now I was too late. I worried about how I would farm and tend the flock. Whence I would get the wherewithal. Somehow, I have managed to put one foot in front of the other. Sarah says the Lord provides. I have had to study the Word with diligence, so I may open its truths. Reading the German does not come hard. But I must commit to memory whole passages so that I may hold forth from the heart. When I cut up felled timber, I practice reciting aloud what I have studied the night before. Sometimes my voice gives out and I become hoarse from the exercise. Sarah says not to strain or I will only squeak.

Seeking after the right words. What a burden! These are sorely trying times. Our settlement here in Somerset County demands a heavy price with its stubborn rocks and wild animals. This last attack on our safety, the murder of the Hershberger baby, reminds us that our trials and tribulations will not soon end. More of our number may depart soon, as word spreads of a more tillable land to the west. Yet, there are those like me who shrink from adventure. Sarah and I are barely making a start at home-steading. We were thankful for better yields last summer. We have our five and if the Lord wills, we will put more at the table. Sarah knows well how to kindle me.

But this Kiss that has fallen to me remains heavy and beset with snares. I do not want to escape to the West, but neither do I want to tend the burdens at my door. Sarah says to pray for wisdom. I am not the one to mend this contention between brothers. I fear I will need Bishop Blauch's help with discernment. I do not want to choose sides. Yet, one of my appoint-ments is to keep the church pure. Without spot or wrinkle. "Protect and establish what is good; punish and hinder what is evil." That is one thing to hear. It is another thing to know how to do.

If the lines fall in the direction of shunning, the hornet's nest buzzes in my mind again. The intent is for the sinner to seek to be received back into the church. As a member in good standing. There is no clearer way for the wayward man to see his error. If you separate a cow from the rest of the herd, she bawls to be let back in. But my inclination is to

shrink from difficult tasks. I am no good as a Gate
Keeper. It is not only the Hershberger case that
buzzes. People come and go all the time. In and out of
the settlement. In and out of the church. There is too
much movement to keep track of. Yet, we ministers
all agreed at last fall's conference: all who leave the
Amish Church and join others are to be regarded as
apostate and considered as subjects for the ban. How
easy to agree; how hard to enforce. This practice of
the *Meidung*. The ban, as we say today. I can only
shake my head. Not that I am opposed. Only, that I
am not the man. Brother Blauch explains with ease:
the *Meidung* is why we have our Amish Church. Our
Brother Ammann, Jakob Ammann, discerned the drift
from teaching the ban among the Mennonites in
Europe years ago. Now we must have courage. Like
unto Ammann's. To do the Lord's bidding and seek to
hold the line. Ammann is right. When we adhere to
these teachings, we have peace and contentment. But
I am not the man. I do not like the feel of the whip in
my hand. Let someone else do it.

I have studied the Word. I have read the Dordrecht
Confession of Faith, dear to Brother Ammann. But let
someone else pull the string across the door. I fear
that my reproof could lead to a brother's ruin instead
of his amendment. That is why I turn away. I do not
want to make an enemy of a brother. Sarah promises
that the Lord will show the way. The erring brother
will return to the fold. But I know how weak is this
poor servant. If it were hers to do, she might hesitate
also.

I keep my thoughts steeped in Scripture. That is the
only way to know how to admonish both the fallen

and the righteous. When I strike the froe with my sledge, I say the words of our brother Paul: "Now the Lord of peace himself give you peace always by all means. The Lord be with you all." Yes, I have memorized these words, written first to the Thessalonians. Sarah reminds me to include the h sound. I am prone to say only Tessalonians. Peace always. That is the promise.

Evelyn Miller is an English professor and writer in Jefferson, Wisconsin.

Surprised

by Sarah Klassen

Erica's colleagues at North-East Life Assurance would be astonished to see her down on all fours in torn jeans, her brown hair in disarray, fingernails dirty.

"That's not like Erica," they might say, and someone would add, facetiously, "Is she praying?"

Someone else would venture, "Need a hand up, Erica?"

But of course, none of her colleagues are anywhere near. At five o'clock they tidied their desks, and on the elevator down reminded each other of urgent messages to be sent first thing in the morning, potential contacts to be tracked down, deadlines to be met. Everything connected somehow with insuring or assuring life.

The pressing need to insure life is far from Erica's mind, though her cell phone is jammed into her jeans pocket. Nor is she looking for a hand up. She is kneeling in her garden a few feet from the six tomato plants she set out last week and somewhat farther from the poppies that have begun the transformation from tight green buds to audacious orange blooms. Although her position might suggest humility and petition, Erica is not praying. She is running her slender, manicured fingers back and forth, back and forth through the black soil looking for a cutworm.

Her bent knees flank a cucumber seedling splayed on the sun-baked earth. Just yesterday—newly planted, fertilized, watered—it stood as upright and green as its three sister seedlings. Today Erica found it sheared off just below the soil, the leaves limp and losing color. When she finds the culprit responsible for this devastation she will kill it. Then she will return to the house, where her daughter has upped the volume on her CD player so the beat of the Backstreet Boys pounds in every room.

"Turn that down," she'll yell.

Diane, at 13, has turned sullenness into a strategy that she hones through constant practice. Music provides the cover. She turned up the Backstreet Boys to annoy her mother, though it wasn't music they disagreed about today, but the movie "Drives." Diane's friends are going after supper, why can't she?

"Over my dead body," Erica said, and Diane shot back with: "It's the mind that dies first." She will not come out of her room or turn down the volume until she is good and ready.

She is lying on her bed, staring at the ceiling. When that becomes tedious, she scans the walls. Amidst posters of the Spice Girls, Keannu Reeves, in-your-face slogans, her eyes come to rest on a modest incongruity, almost lost in the collage of color and gloss and celebrity. A cross-stitched motto in a narrow frame announces: "I am the Resurrection and the Life." It was a birthday gift from her grandmother, two years ago. Not a gift she received with much enthusiasm then, nor one she particularly prizes now. Whenever

Gigi or Aynsley or Judy enter the room Diane gets nervous and hopes they won't notice it. It would be so embarrassing. Once she took it down and hid it, but afterwards she returned it to its place.

From her prone position she scrutinizes the exquisite stitching and the ornate cross superimposed on the "I." Her grandmother who made those perfect stitches has become an old, helpless woman. Diane can't imagine anyone being so motionless. She wonders if her grandmother who once quilted and made pickles and was always generous with homemade cookies was ever as unreasonable as her mother has become.

The Backstreet Boys blare into her ear.

Erica is determined to find the cutworm. Later this evening she will visit her mother in Resthaven. She'll bring a bunch of poppies, a guilt offering for not coming oftener. The poppies are amazing. When it's the season for blooming, nothing can stop them. At North-East Life Assurance everything depends on human effort; here in the garden, growth happens almost in spite of it. Nothing can stop the weeds. And worms.

Erica experienced her first cutworm in her mother's garden, when she was younger than Diane is now. "Just move the earth around the fallen plant, gently," her mother instructed. "Likely the worm's overstuffed from chomping through the stem and can't move far." Sure enough, the worm was easily found and destroyed, though it was her mother, not Erica, who killed that first one, demonstrating how it was done. Gross, Diane would say.

Erica keeps looking.

Two nurses are bent over a thin old woman curled tight and small in her white hospital bed, her eyes closed, her breathing almost imperceptible.

"You grab the top, I'll get the bottom," one of them says.

"Poor old thing," the other replies. They take hold of shoulders and buttocks, turning the old woman cautiously onto her other side. They tug at the bed clothes and try to rearrange the stiff limbs.

"Pain, Granny?" They hover uncertainly over the bed.

The slight motion of the woman's head could be yes, could be no.

"Bye then, Sweetheart." They hurry off.

The fetal woman is not the oldest in the nursing home, but perhaps the most pathetic. Her muscles have atrophied; she needs help with everything. Every movement is painful and speaking is such a huge effort, she seldom attempts it. Sometimes the nurses assume mistakenly that there's as little activity in the mind as in the body.

The woman, cocooned in bedsheets and pain, is imagining the world beyond this small white room. That world is hazy, as if someone has pulled a veil over it. Or as if it is receding, and she sees it from a distance. She is vaguely aware that it's spring, and the grey winter trees have taken on the pale green of the season.

She has known for some time now that she's no longer necessary. Spring will pass without her seeing it. But her daughter will see it. And her granddaughter. She pictures them in a garden, surrounded in a shimmer of flowering shrubs and birdsong, breathing in the scent of lilies and mock orange. The wind riffles their

hair; they lift their faces to the sun. The old woman
believes she can see them turn to each other and smile
and her face too twists into a kind of smile.

And then the muted tones and shades of the garden
give way to vivid colors and music of startling clarity.
Everything around and inside the old woman vibrates
with light. And with anticipation. Her limbs begin
unfolding and she is amazed to find herself growing,
not larger, but lighter. And free of pain. Any minute
now she will rise like the fluffy seed of cottonwood that
in June floats on the air and is carried on the wind's
breath to every corner of the garden.

"Looked like she was smiling," one nurse observed
afterwards.

"Surprised," the other thought.

Just when Erica is ready to give up on the cutworm,
there it is. An inch long, thick, and the color of earth.
Gorged with chewed cucumber stem, it lies inert,
stretched out to its full stubby length. There is no curl-
ing up for protection. No hint of resistance. Erica is
caught off guard, as though she has come upon it unex-
pectedly. She is surprised by its utter helplessness and
momentarily distracted, but not deterred from taking
the creature to the sidewalk, and stomping down on it
hard with the heel of her Reebok.

"They're tough," her mother used to say. "If you
don't do a good job on them, they'll recover. They'll kill
more of your plants. They'll spin a cocoon and become
a moth and come next spring—the whole business all
over again."

Erica has no time to ponder the unstoppable urge,
evident everywhere in her garden, to keep on being

and growing. Before she returns to the house, to her adolescent daughter and the blaring CD, she surveys once more the six sturdy tomato plants and the three remaining cucumber seedlings. Then she strides, purposefully, toward the unbridled orange poppies.

Diane is considering whether her life will be worth living, or even possible, if she doesn't get to see "Drives." What will she tell Gigi, Aynsley, Judy? So embarrassing to have a dull, narrow-minded mother. The afternoon sun pours into her room. She is bored and hungry. She reaches over to turn down the Backstreet Boys.

When she enters the kitchen, heading for the fridge, her mother is there in front of it, half-hidden by a shocking orange blaze.

"Oh my God," Diane gasps.

"I'm taking them to Granny's, right after supper," Erica says. "Want to come?"

Diane stares at the stunning orange blaze that fills the kitchen, demanding her attention, crowding out every other sensation. She considers her mother's invitation, considers rejecting it bcause she's going to a movie, but her eyes are fixed on the poppies, their brilliant authority.

"Why not." She shrugs. "Granny will sure be surprised."

Erica is about to agree but her cell phone rings and her free hand, recently in contact with black soil and with a worm's cold skin, reaches quickly for it.

Sarah Klassen, Winnipeg, Manitoba, is a poet, writer, and editor.

By the Editors

I. M. Good
Memories of My Father
by Merle Good

As I write this, my father is quietly, peacefully slipping from life. His physical health has been failing for quite a while and he has been steadily losing his memory for a number of years. They give him "a few hours to a few months" to live. He does not appear to be in much pain or distress, just easing back into his childhood in a bittersweet ending which mirrors his beginning.

My father was a much-loved pastor who made his livelihood as a farmer. So stories from farm life and nature and favorite scriptures and hymns still bring a spark to his eyes as he lies in his bed in the nursing home. His sense of humor is still there, too, as well as that gracious spirit which served him so well during his 87 years.

It feels as though I've been grieving the loss of Dad for many years, yet I'm sure that I'll miss him dreadfully when he crosses over. He has probably been the most influential person in shaping my life, and time and again I find myself quoting something he has said.

"Show interest" was one of his soft-spoken encouragements as we seven boys were growing up. (Sorry, no sisters.) In whatever situation you find yourself, show interest in those around you. Don't be a big shot, don't think you're better than others. Open your eyes, show interest, and life will be so much more rewarding. It still seems like good advice for young people, and for older ones as well. Take the effort and learn the humility to show interest in others, all others. Rather Christian, really.

Another of Dad's sentiments was "We'll do our best, but if we don't get it done today, there's always tomorrow." Not lazy, mind you, not haphazard. But realistically relaxed about pace in life. Being super-rich or super-busy had little appeal for Dad. Be a good steward of life, resources, time. But don't be obsessive, don't go crazy trying to be the best or accomplish the most. Enjoy life and learn your measure.

"Learn to be balanced" was something Dad said more than once. Avoid extremes. As Mennonites, we knew that some of our beliefs and practices (nonconformity and nonresistance) might seem extreme to other Christians. But within the Mennonite flow of things, Dad sought moderation. He was a peacemaker, seeking common ground for whatever the issue. Learn to live in harmony with others. Dad illustrated a mode of listening rather than debating, something his family and his congregation benefitted from. Not that he was wishy-washy; he was solid as a rock. But he knew how to be secure in his belief without needing to commandeer the situation.

Dad was not enamored of higher education and degrees, any more that he was by lots of money. Dad learned to speak English as a child by going to school, the Pennsylvania Dutch dialect being the language in his Mennonite home. And he completed only eight grades.

But he was always curious, always learning. After the lot for minister fell on him, he became more studious, buying books, attending a few Bible classes, and spending a great deal of time with the Bible. I remember one time as a teenager, travelling all night to get home from a trip and, arriving home before five in the morning, finding Dad in our farm kitchen, reading his Bible, as he did every morning for a half hour or more before heading to the cowstable.

Not that Dad opposed higher education; he saw it as a slippery slope of sorts. Learning is fine, but letting degrees warp your sense of who you are is as dangerous to a Christian as letting millions of dollars shape your identity. Learn—but also learn to be humble.

Was Dad smart enough to get an advanced degree, if he had given his heart to it? Of course. Could he have leveraged the farm into an agricultural empire of sorts? Sure. Was his heart in that? No. He lived a modest life, close to farm and family and devoted to the church.

About the church. Dad was a bit skeptical about big meetings and big church institutions and organizations. He was slow to run off to hear speakers and attend rallies. His heart was in the congregation and, like his bishop/farmer father before him, he had deep appreciation for Lancaster Conference.

Dad always told us boys, "We don't go to church to be important; we go to church to serve." He encouraged us, "Whatever they ask you to do at church, regardless of how seemingly unimportant, don't say no unless you have a really good reason. Always be ready to serve."

There was a time Dad didn't follow his own advice.

When the district was receiving nominations for bishop, he begged people not to nominate him. They did anyhow, but much to his relief, the lot did not fall on him.

Another thing Dad would say is that we should learn to give thanks, regardless of our situation. There will be plentiful harvests, but there will also be drought. Learn to be thankful in all situations. For me that's been the most difficult of his encouragements to accept.

Dad hasn't lived a perfect life, of course. In spite of modesty and moderation being his watchwords, he did enjoy a bit of flair. His wit brought many smiles; even now, lying in his bed, remembering little of the days he's lived since 1914, he still brings a smile to the faces of his visitors. In addition to his wit, he showed his flair in that little extra length he liked in his hair, just enough to let the wave show at the back of his beautiful bald head.

And of course, there was the bit about his name. Ira Mathias Good. He was known as Ira, but he used his initials in a lot of official documents, even on our mailbox at the end of the lane. I never heard anyone criticize him for doing so. In a way, it was nonoffensive to see such a modest man sign his name as "I. M. Good." And to a great many persons, including some of our unchurched neighbors, he *was* a good man.

In any case, I've always been modestly proud to be the son of I. M. Good. He was not a famous preacher, not a super-rich farmer. He and Mother raised seven sons who are all still in the church, though all but one have left the farm. But it was the accent of his life, the tone of graciousness, the moderation and showing interest in others that made him such a good man. In need of God's grace, he would quickly add.

I hope that when my time comes to cross over, I can feel such peace and hope as I see in my father. I hope the memory of his encouragements and the example of his generous life will stay always in my mind, as a conscience and a comfort for my way.

Merle Good of Lancaster, Pennsylvania, is a writer, dramatist, publisher, and a co-editor of this volume.

Tiny Tempest—
Amish Quilts and the Color Guard

by Phyllis Pellman Good

Are symbols free for the taking? Might we need a little protocol here, perhaps some small "people's bench" who would look at certain sneaky occasions of symbol piracy?

Here's what happened. This summer the United States Postal Service decided to issue a set of postage stamps for first-class mail featuring antique Amish quilts. Four quilts were selected; each image repeated five times on a panel of 20 34-cent stamps—a Diamond in the Square (made around 1920), a Lone Star (also made about 1920), a Sunshine and Shadow (made circa 1910), and a Double Ninepatch Variation (made about 1940).

The USPS used these patchwork wonders to kick off their "American Treasures" series; presumably more folk art will follow in later stamp programs. No harm in that, I suppose. The Amish that I know were neither incensed nor impressed. (I am not a totally disinterested party, I must admit. I curate exhibits of antique Amish quilts in our quilt museum, edit and write quilt books, and help to direct an educational center about the Amish.)

It did seem to me that the Amish—without anyone asking their permission, of course—had inched further toward finding a place on the Shelf of American Icons, reserved for colorful, charming curios incapable of causing disturbance, but certain to bring comfort and pride to spectators.

Then I attended the "Second Day Ceremony." Despite the fact that these four graphic beauties were made in Lancaster, Pennsylvania, the USPS decided to set its "First Day of Issue Ceremony" in Nappanee, Indiana, where a large arts and crafts festival was already scheduled to be held. The USPS prefers big crowds for its issuing ceremonies, and it found an already-made one in northern Indiana that it could be part of. Never mind that these quilts weren't made in that Amish community.

This led to a Big Spat, encouraged by the press in eastern Pennylvania, with even the *Philadelphia Inquirer* crying foul on behalf of Lancaster, its overlooked neighbor. And so Lancaster set about to redress its slight by mounting its own event. At the center, of course, were four boldly colorful Amish quilts, jerked out of their quiet intended use onto a little national stage where they were caught in a tiny tempest.

No Amish attended the Lancaster ceremony. But a color guard did. The first member carried an American flag and the rest of the unit carried guns. They stepped their way to the front of the hall and performed an extended routine involving their symbols of power and patriotism.

None of that diminished the strength and robust simplicity of the four Amish quilts. Their images

shared the platform undeterred with the uniformed
men who came to honor some quiet certainty within
these quilts, and the politicians who came for that—
and to be seen.

So who owns these matchlessly lovely symbols,
these visually stalwart textile statements? I wasn't
really worked up about Indiana being selected as the
site for the issuing event. But my sense of justice
began to simmer when these pieces were poached by
a patriotism which seems so at odds with the people
who made them. Did the officials headlining this ceremony really think that by rubbing up against these
quilts, they could just assume the qualities they represent?

I suppose it's harmless for these people to pay trib-
ute to these monuments of peace and quiet strength.
But should they make them a shrine by employing the
"Star Spangled Banner," guns, and vote-hungry politicians? Probably not.

Here's where we may need the referee. The question is: Who may appropriate which symbols?

In this case, there seems to be no one to ask permission of. The Amish have their Protectors, their
Interpreters, their Liaisons-to-the-Larger-World. They
also have their own Problems Committee. But the
first three of these tribunals have their own agenda,
and the fourth one isn't interested.

And so the Amish, who have long had a sense of
the power of the visual, will go on in spite of their
handiwork being claimed by the politically and mili-
tarily powerful. And the rest of society will keep on
wondering and watching, drawn by these sober people who make startling quilts, uninhibited by decorat-

ing trends or the fear that particular colors don't work together. These are also the people who dress in an unmistakable manner, who drive vehicles that turn heads, and who enlarge their farmhouses (to accommodate their families and their worship services) in ways that confound architectural fashion. In all of these ways the Amish give some hint of their commitments and convictions, expressed in images that stay in the mind. Not the least are their quilts, which state eloquently the bold strength required to live so differently from the society the Amish live among.

So there's probably no need for Symbol Police in this case. Having one of your symbols twisted or misused is a common human hazard, I suppose. Little damage has been done here. The Amish will survive it, and the quilt stamps may only spread the Amish witness further, thanks to the USPS.

Phyllis Pellman Good, Lancaster, Pennsylvania, is a writer, editor, and co-editor of this collection.

Poetry, I

Green Man in
Good Neighborhood

by Rhoda Janzen

I

At 3:30 a.m. the guest bathroom fidgets
fever, ghostly and unfamiliar. Veins
marble the skin, nonfat-blue on white,
otherworldly as a formica countertop.
It is the parents' house. The climate
offers one damp hand, a stranger. Windows
yawn all night; July is a late show through
which one seeks to sleep. Outside a soapsud
moon cleans all the world above Al Pauls'
garage. Homes along this block square
shoulders at lawns so stiffly green.

II

The ferns look like topiary cough drops,
snug Sucrets, low as a cough suppressed
in church—the same church just around
the corner with its faint quiet threat
of Sundays. That afternoon, still feeling fine,
one might recline on the dense shaved lawn
and seduce Al Pauls' cat to rub one's thigh.
The shadow of the kumquat tempts

illustration, an ancient edifice whose
bas-relief's been blunted over time.

III

The linoleum's hardly to your taste
and the wallpaper gallops minatory florals—
it shouts, it husks, it swings you round.
It whirls some dervish dance when in fact
one cannot stand. Because the bathroom's
adjacent to the parents' room, eventually
the mother's hand taps the door
like a root, pushing through cranapple
and immodium. She apologizes
for the rich cream sauce at supper.
How regrettable to have admitted a lack
of emotion altogether! "What about fear,"
she asks. "What about Satan?" Once
blackened hoary calluses goatfooted it
down the hall; razors puzzled cold
configurations. Recall the dreamstop
of the deep red eye. You sadly shake
your head, though you aren't sad. You
have no fear of Satan, nor thrill of God, nor
love of man. Even now the twisting of your
trunk as you lean unsound into your sickness

IV

shoots a fuzz of seedlings. Pale ribs petrify
a casement with carved medieval cornice:
the Green Man, from whose lips emerge
vines that creep and bloom above his head,

WHAT MENNONITES ARE THINKING, 2001

looping into frenetic Latin. Throbbing cutworms,
tendrils inch out of Green Man's ears,
and his eyes cry leaves and buds of leaves.
Lean your forehead on the window, which
although not cool is cooler than your skin.
From the parents' screen a conversation
is spreading, a low voice rich as loam
and a softer, white-magnolia voice against it.
Pinch your forehead and feel for pain.
If in the refulgent furrow between your brows
you detect a swell, a nub rising, a sprig
of fragrant lavender, they had best let you go

to the lawn and the cat and Al Pauls' moon,
where with care from the gardening crew
your limbs will extend a pergola, on which
you will sustain seasons and echoes of seasons
with the riots that sweep into spring,
the purple shouting masses of hysteria.

*Rhoda Janzen, Holland, Michigan, is a poet and professor
teaching creative writing.*

Table Prayer

by Keith Ratzlaff

My grandmother has a canary
blind in one eye
that sings as if the world

had just one blue window
framing a garden,
and one bad picture—this one

hanging above his cage
in the dining room—
of Christ, ghostly and plasmic

helping a sailor steer
his ship
through a gale.

The weather's rough, buckets
plunging overboard,
halyards running away

on the wind. Soon, Christ or no,
this one's going down.
The canary doesn't know this;

WHAT MENNONITES ARE THINKING, 2001

it's not his job. But
I'm a sinner
when I sit at her table,

and I play the drama out
during the drone
of grace: *Kommt Herr Jesu* . . .

I'm a sailor on that ship,
a bit player
flung heavily overboard

into the scud and dark
obsidian water.
Then the wreck's petals

scattering on the shore.
Then sharks,
so my lost soul

is both eaten and drowned.
But *amen* and
I am in the eternal now

of family dinners: saved
by white bread
and beef and canned beans.

The canary's song is muffled
under the towel
we've put over the cage

to shut him up. Grandma's old.
God is real to her
if not perfect. She loves

the metaphor of sailing,
the rocking
and spray. The continuous moment

of never going down
is what
being saved means to her.

Oh Lord come be our guest.
Bless us,
keep us from your harm.

Keep the bird quiet.
Give us
your grace, which is like

these pickles, which are like
last year's,
God-awful and abundant

world without end. Amen.

Keith Ratzlaff is a poet and professor in Pella, Iowa.

Rhapsody with Dark Matter

by Jeff Gundy

What's moving on the hills could be mist or rain
the first long notes of the apocalypse

or just another load of thick summer dreams.
What's coming won't be hurried or put off.

Yes the stars are out there, blazing, and all
the dark matter too. A woman with son and daughter

settles in beneath a bridge, smooths cardboard
with a dirty hand. A man pours beer and brags

of the tank he drove into the desert. Two million
    bucks.
So much easier to blow things up than get them right,

a marriage, a country, a small town forty miles
from the nearest beer. It isn't just this poem

that's loose, gliding from scenery to disaster,
floating through the gorgeous, deadly world.

It's not just me. Say what you will about the dark—
it won't leave you contented, or alone. It saunters

at its own pace down the long bluff, up the streets
of the finest little town in Arkansas. I'm trying
to remember where the keys are, which road I'll take
out of town. Remembering a voice: *I'm tired, yes.*

The boys are fine. Call Tuesday. Bring yourself home.

*Jeff Gundy is a poet and professor living and writing in
Bluffton, Ohio.*

What I Stole

by Cheryl Denise

was a Sunday School globe.
It was a little bigger than a baseball.
The oceans were bright blue
and Canada was red
Australia and New Zealand were purple.

Mrs. Snyder told us we should tithe our allowance.
She pointed to Nigeria and said
the money was to feed kids just like us
who liked to climb trees and play hide-n-seek
only these kids hadn't enough to eat.
Matthew asked if they didn't have grandmothers.

We filled the world with our nickels and dimes
at the beginning of class.
Later Mrs. Snyder put them in an envelope
dated it, marked our attendance
and checked the grade one box
tied the clamps and slid it under the door.

While she read about Jesus
feeding five thousand
we could hear John in the hall
collecting envelopes.
He got to open them and count the money
and send it to the kids.

What I Stole

I kept thinking how good the globe would look
on my dresser
I could learn where Sudan, Zimbabwe and the Gold
    Coast were.
I wondered if the oceans were really that blue
and did they turn paler at the edges?
Was the dirt under my house red?
I was sure this was how God made the world.

After class, after everyone left
I slipped the globe under my dress.

I hid it in my sock drawer
too afraid to take it out much
and learn my countries
and think what it would have been like
to live in a green or yellow place.

The next Sunday
Mrs. Snyder said the globe was missing
and she hoped whoever took it would bring it back
that we needed it to feed the children.
I thought we could just put the money in the envelope.

I couldn't figure a way to get it back
without anyone seeing me.
I could just imagine my classmates
Shannon and Charlotte laughing.

WHAT MENNONITES ARE THINKING, 2001

It was no fun playing with the globe.
When spring came
I wrapped it in an old T-shirt
threw it in the trash.
And I remember thinking
how much better it would have been
to steal bubble gum
or bottle cap candies from Stedmans.

Cheryl Denise is a poet living in Philippi, West Virginia.

Markings

by Jean Janzen

They come home with school papers flapping
in their hands, wings for civilization.
They smell like wind,

grounded in their bodies. I kiss them,
admire the strokes, the rows
of o's, save the best from year to year,

like the layered leaf-fall. Like
the botany booklet of my school years,
the pages filled with the wet green

of summer's trees—maple, box elder,
        ash, and that catalpa leaf which I loved,
its thick veins, the way it overfilled

the page. Oh, I know it will all be buried,
pressed into rock at last. And yet,
somehow those markings loosen out of time.

What the children printed, bold—
*Yesterday I caught a dragonfly,
and then I let it go*—is saved, somewhere,

WHAT MENNONITES ARE THINKING, 2001

the place we enter after death.
That book of leaves.
And on the front, our names.

Jean Janzen is a poet living and writing in Fresno,
California.

The Amateur

by David Waltner-Toews

The woman in front of me
at the bank machine
turns sideways and disappears.
"Must be one of those ballerinas or gymnasts,"
I remark to the man behind me,
"a real pro."
He is staring at where I should be
and I realize: he can't see me
from this angle. I pirouette
and guffaw. Seeing me now, he knows
I am an amateur,
and intently checks his pocket organizer
for missed appointments.

In this city of homo economicus,
abstracticus, bottom-line-icus,
everywhere, on the bus,
at the office, canadicus, francoamericanus,
anti or pro, this is the crime:
that a man can still be amateur,
uncertain, seen, obscenely, from all angles,
practicing at his humanity, asking
what it means, that he can offer flowers,
make faces at the baby in the grocery cart,
dig into his pockets for change at the cashier,
have to put back the cookies,

WHAT MENNONITES ARE THINKING, 2001

that he might try his hand
at baking a pie with fresh-sliced apples,
bloody his finger at the counter,
at the end of a long day at the office
make a mess of supper,
raise a glass of wine,
say something utterly inappropriate,
crudely sexual, religious, political,
some gut feeling surfacing,
the soul's loch monster gasping for air,
or speak of rainy evenings
and empty streets at dawn,
or, without irony, lament his success,
or cry in the bathroom,
for no reason he can think of,
or laugh at Saturday cartoons.

And everywhere, standing in line at the grocery store,
looking up from a pile of papers
in some professor's office,
or drunk, begging a loonie for coffee in front of the bank,
there are people in this city
without poems, their own poems,
in this city where books are balanced,
not read or celebrated,
when everywhere the words are trashed,
tongue-lashed, and trod upon,
when so little is required
to fashion a few lines, to weave a garland
from the litter
of our daily speech, a gift for having lived
another day amid the fragile, happy

babble of a family, the info-streets strewn
with the pulp and wreckage of our public cant,

so little to dream on, to suckle hope's gaunt baby.

Take these lines. Take these lines,
these unpeeled syllables left lying
on the table, next to an empty glass,
next to a flag, just another colored napkin,
red and white blue and white, whatever,
in the silence, right there
at the Interac, at the checkout,
cup them in your hands,
hum a tune for no reason,
turn yourself around and around and
all around you, homo categoricus,
pigeon holicus, will stare at you
suddenly, brashly, blushingly visible.

You can feel them in your palm
like tiny squabs
scrabbling for crumbs.

David Waltner-Toews, Kitchener, Ontario, is a professor,
veterinary epidemiologist, and poet.

Featured Articles,
Essays, and Opinions, II

The Child Bride

by Janet Toews Berg

"The bride isn't feeling very well." Dad's words take me completely by surprise as I enter the church precisely at 2:30 p.m., the time scheduled for Photograph of Musicians on the wedding agenda. My thoughts begin to race both forward and back as we walk together to the front of the church to assess the situation. I had finally become friends with the idea that Violet and Kenton really *were* going to get married. Now this. What if Violet is too sick to go through with it? Maybe everything will have to be canceled. Maybe everyone will finally realize what I have known all along—Violet is simply too young to get married.

When my little sister called six months ago to say that she and Kenton were planning to get married, I was too stunned to protest. I agreed to sing and even made immediate train reservations to arrive in eastern Montana on July 21, the wedding rehearsal day. Yes, I went along with it at the time because I had met her boyfriend, Kenton, and he struck me as being very nice.

But so young! Violet must be about 12, and Kenton maybe 13 or 14. I have no trouble remembering Violet's birth. I was a senior in high school when Mother came into the room I shared with my 15-year-old sister, and with a red face asked us if we could keep a secret for awhile. I felt embarrassed picturing

a pregnant mother at my graduation, but figured all
would be forgotten by my friends when they saw me
expertly handling a newborn baby that first Sunday in
church. As it turned out, I never got the change to
show off at church. The baby was due in early August
but was not born until August 27. My mother and the
baby were still in the hospital the last Sunday before I
left for college. My father announced the news this
way, "This is a special time for our family. Our oldest
daughter is leaving for college this week. Fortunately,
we have gotten a replacement."

During those first weeks of college I had little time
to think about my replacement, but when meeting
new people I enjoyed the gasps of amazement when I
said I was one of nine children and that my youngest
sister was one week old. Periodically I had to advance
Violet's age given the amount of time I had been
away. Maybe I haven't kept up very well, but I *know* I
haven't been away from home long enough for her to
be getting married.

I had no idea what to expect when we arrived in
Montana yesterday. Who would be in charge? Six
months ago we gathered here for our mother's funeral. It was strangely comfortable then. Mom had been
disabled for years and had been in a nursing home for
a year before her death. We had all grieved many
times over the years, and the funeral was simply a
final ceremony of Mom's life. Dad was completely in
charge then, but I couldn't expect him to do the same
for his daughter's wedding. All of us older siblings
were married, and most lived too far away to be
involved. "This could be a disaster," a negative
thought whispered.

My first surprise was the rehearsal dinner. We arrived at the church late, thanks to Amtrak's "special summer schedule," and thought we would join a meal in progress; it was only family, wasn't it? How I had underestimated someone! This meal was organized. They had waited for us, we all sat down at the same time, and there were place cards. Before we were finished eating, Violet and Kenton stood up (all by themselves without anyone telling them to) and introduced everyone. Who were all these people? Oh yes, some were Kenton's family from North Dakota. But did I hear Kansas? Some came from as far away as Kansas? Especially for this wedding?

The rehearsal took me completely off guard. I expected a quick run-through of the sequence of the wedding, and then we musicians could practice our music. I was wrong. After a brief introduction and prayer by the pastor, we were each given a photo-copied sheet which resembled the script for a play. As I scanned it, my knees went weak. There was my name on it and stage directions. I was to sit *L FRONT ROW, fourth from the end.* My first directions were: *Janet stands up as Kenton gets all the way out . . . Janet sings . . .* My thoughts were racing, "I should have been here a week ago. I'll bet they have all been rehearsing this play for a week, and I have gone over my songs with the accompanist exactly once. When I consented to sing, somehow I thought someone would just nod to me when it was time to sing. Now I can see that everyone else has their own parts to memorize and I am on my own."

I began to panic. "What if I should stand up *before* Kenton gets all the way out, would I ruin everything?

What if I didn't see him getting out and forgot to stand up? What then? Would they go on without my song? And by the way, where was Kenton going? And how would I know when he was *all* the way out?" I managed to calm myself as Pastor Chett began reading the script aloud from the beginning, explaining first that the bride and groom wrote their own wedding.

I had heard about couples writing their own weddings, and I'm sure that some of our college friends did. Al and I got married between semesters in medical school, so we used a standard service offered by the Presbyterian church I was attending at the time. The pastor was in charge of the rehearsal a half hour before the service.

For all I can remember, some of my other brothers and sisters may have written their own weddings, too. But they were not children like Violet and Kenton. Despite my denial, I could not ignore the numerous occasions that Pastor Chett asked, "Violet and Kenton, how do you want this done?" Each time they answered with what sounded like the authority of authors. I could not escape the truth; they wrote this wedding program!

We rehearsed the entire program twice, and then Pastor Chett sat us down to go over what turned out to be my third surprise: the Wedding Day Schedule. I could not believe what I was hearing. The wedding was to be at 4:00 p.m., but the agenda started at 1:30. A simple mental calculation told me that those who were being photographed at 1:30 would have to start getting ready at 12:30. When the pastor had finished going over the schedule, I wanted to raise my hand and ask, "What about lunch?" and "What about naps?"

But Pastor Chett did not ask if anyone had questions. No one else seemed concerned about these glaring omissions in the wedding day schedule. "Maybe you're the one that's getting older," buzzed another negative thought through my mind. Yes; I had turned 40 about three months ago and decided that naps were a good thing for everyone.

After rehearsal, everyone seemed to be going home. True, it was almost 9:30 p.m. and I was tired. But I was also bursting with the need for private family conversation. Why was everyone so serious and obedient. Didn't anyone have the same need to discuss this whole event? Was everyone simply going home to study their scripts? Reluctantly, I followed my husband and our four-year-old daughter to our assigned place for the night. We didn't have far to go; we were at the parsonage just across the church yard.

At 10:00 p.m. there was a knock on the pastor's door, and I heard my sister Ellen's voice saying something about decorating at the church and whether Janet wanted to come and help. Suddenly I was no longer tired, and I signaled to her from the bedroom doorway that I would be right over as soon as I tucked Clara into bed. Al wondered why this couldn't wait till morning? I knew there was no way of explaining to him that "decorating" was only the code word for visiting, and since the rehearsal was so serious, we had had no time to talk.

As I picked my way over to the church in the warm darkness, I felt confident that Ellen would feel the same way I did about Violet being too young. She was a sophomore in high school when Violet was born. She was ecstatic at the news of Mom's pregnancy. "I felt like heaven opened and dumped blessings right on my head," she often said. She was only seven when the last baby, Karen, was born, too young to be included in the secret as I was, and too old to bond with the baby as a playmate. Having her annoying older sister replaced with a baby was a Heavenly Dumping indeed. But now surely any differences in our feelings had to take second place to the imminent loss of our baby sister to the young man from North Dakota.

Alas, I was surprised again when I got to the church to find family members not visiting, but seriously decorating. Not only that, but my sister Ellen was directing the efforts. Why was she not having a hard time with this? No one seemed interested in talking, so I got to work twisting crepe paper streamers and doing some mental math. If I had recently turned 40, and I was 18 when Violet was born, how old would that make her? Rounding off the numbers, she could be close to 20. But no, she and Kenton both graduated from Tabor College just two months ago. Was it possible she was nearly 22? It still seemed too young, but just because I waited until I was 26 to get married was no reason to doom her to wait.

With that worked out, and with the benefits of a good night's sleep, breakfast, lunch *and* a nap, I arrived at the church at 2:30 p.m. with a whole new attitude. Now I am completely confused by Dad's news of Violet not feeling well. This was not in the script. This is real life! Violet's age is no longer the issue; what she needs now is a big sister.

I go into action. Together my husband and I assess that Violet is feeling the combined effects of the heat (it is about 90 degrees in the church and rising), not having eaten lunch ("tut tut, what did I tell you," I want to say, but I stop myself), dehydration, and nervousness. I go through my ministrations: drink orange juice, keep close to the fan, sit as much as possible. Somehow we get through the photographs. I have placed two chairs just outside the platform area, a pitcher of water nearby, and have given instructions to my fellow musicians and the minister to bring out the chairs at the first sign of a faint or the Meditation, whichever comes first.

Four o'clock sharp. I am in my place among the other musicians, front left, fourth from the end. I can do no more. This is it. Violet is on her own (come to think of it, we are all on our own; any one of us could faint, this heat is stifling!). My heart pounds as the ushers light the candles. What is my cue again? *Janet sings after Kenton gets all the way out . . .* Here he comes already, ushering in his parents. How handsome and confident he looks. He could be 20.

The wedding is going exactly as we rehearsed it. I see the minister now and then asking Violet something, presumably if she wants to sit down, but she refuses and we move on. The meditation, the music, and now the vows, and no adolescent prayers are these that Kenton and Violet pray with surprisingly strong voices. I am forced to advance their ages far ahead of what I gave them credit for yesterday. I find myself relaxing and the damp Kleenex in my hand is beginning to dry.

"I now introduce to you Mr. and Mrs. Kenton Vix." There, it is over. I cannot believe it. We made it. We go downstairs to the cool basement as soon as the

ushers let us. I expect that now Violet and Kenton
will collapse and sit in relief. What? They're planning
to stand through the entire reception line to greet all
the people? Kids don't listen to reason these days. I
start to tut, tut again. Then I have to remind myself,
"You are old enough to be her mother. But you must
stop thinking of her as your child." Yes, I must. I relax
and go back to the wedding cake and ham sandwich
on my plate. And I must keep track of my own
daughter, Clara, who was a few minutes ago playing
hide-and-seek under the communion table.

I have one last misgiving. One last Big Sister worry.
The Going Away. My daughter excitedly pulls on my
hand, "Mommy, come and see Kenton and Violet's
car. It's all decorated!" Decorated was not the word I
would have used; messed up was more like it. My
heart sinks. The doors are tied shut with string, there
are marshmallows and Oreo cookies smeared all over
it, and the engine, rumor has it, is "fixed up" so it will
not start. How can they do this to a couple of kids
who have been through so much already? Here they
come, still in their wedding clothes, and Violet still
glowing with health (either that long time of standing
and shaking hands didn't hurt her or some wedding
cake and punch revived her).

This time it is Kenton who amazes me: no anger,
no frustration. He calmly pulls a pair of scissors out
of his pocket, cuts the strings, wipes the marshmallows off the door handles, and in they go. He starts
the car as easily as can be, and they drive away amid
the rattle of tin cans and shouts of children.

I turn and meet the eyes and arms of my sister
Ellen who says out loud what I have been thinking all

day, "There goes our baby sister." We laugh and cry and hug and then compose ourselves. She agrees with me; we have to stop thinking of Violet as a little girl. I reach for my daughter's hand to go back into the church where it is cooler. "Come Violet, let's go," I hear myself say.

Janet Toews Berg is a psychiatrist and writer in Seattle, Washington.

Confessions of a Hutterite Convert

by Robert Rhodes

Touchstone magazine had a cover story the other month on "pugnacious converts"—spiritual gadflies who come to roost in one religious milieu or another, explore and praise its many virtues, and then proceed to famously rock the boat with vigor and effect. We all know the sort: Augustine, Merton, and certainly the figures of the Reformation. Though I am a convert to the Hutterites, which is nearly unheard of, I dare not class myself with people of such radical mien. However, I guess I'm pugnacious in my own way, and my family's presence in a colony of the Hutterian Brethren likely rocks more boats than not.

Not that we try. But this is what going against tradition will get for you, and tradition is something Hutterites eagerly embrace.

We came to the Hutterites because we felt God was asking something more of us than living conventional, if faithful or meaningful, lives in the greater society. To do such a thing is to answer a distinct call, a call that not everyone hears. To answer such a call is also to embrace a certain contradiction: Why apartness and not activism? Why this and not something else? Perhaps we should ask instead: What is my true home? What am I called to? Where do I find it?

These we cannot answer rationally, but by drawing near, by hearing the call of the spirit, we can *perceive* them quite plainly.

To live earnestly, as we do, is to live from the ground up, with no illusions and no designs on utopia. We did not join for prosperous times or to chase fair weather. Nor did we join to "find God" amidst our barns and beards and black-centric wardrobe. Instead, we joined the Hutterites because we felt God would like to find us in such a place, not vice versa.

Was this a successful exchange? A life with careers and decent money, for an existence with no private property to speak of, and virtually no say over our own destinies?

Ask me when it's over with, when the people I live and eat with every day take me out to our cemetery, past the tree line and through the wrought-iron gate, and leave me in a six-foot hole, in the homemade coffin that awaits us all. Once I am forgotten, we'll see how pugnacious I really was.

When my family became Hutterites, we realized we were traveling on uncharted ground. Though there had been a few others who had joined from "outside," and many others who had tried but eventually left, we knew there was no simple or even complex path for us to follow. Our entry into this culture—coming from an English-speaking, professional, upper middle-class background, into a German-speaking, Russian-peasant communal background that is strongly familial—was not only a leap of faith, but slightly reckless. We had no idea of the obstacles we would face, and so great was our enthusiasm at first that we tended to ignore the possibility that we might not like what we found.

From this, however, we learned our greatest lesson not only about the Hutterites, but about living in community and living as committed, convicted Christians: There is no easy road. And once you find this path, and discover where it will lead, you cannot turn back unchanged. It is truly, as Job laments, a road of no return.

Man, because of his inner convictions, seeks and cultivates the culture of community. This, because it is basic to man, should be a clear means to a meaningful life, if we do not hinder our communal inclinations. However, because we are human, we seek perfection instead of goodness, and a perfect balance between our faith and practice, instead of a gentle, changing, unbounded harmony. This, because we are awash in faults, is why we will never attain utopia, and why we will always have a terrible struggle on our hands whenever we endeavor to become a community.

Despite the image many have of the Hutterites—of being slightly outdated and less than aware of the nuances of human nature—we have found this to be utterly untrue. I think this is where the Hutterian life has some of its great beauty. After centuries of living in community, with all the ups and downs and tragedies and fallow periods, the Hutterite mind, if such a thing can be said to exist, has become ingrained with the reality of community. It seems, once one truly enters into such a community, that the struggles and hardships of living with other people are so familiar they defy explanation. Our sermons preach it, our immense *Chronicle* recounts it—time and again, the failures and near failures to make community work. Even in communities where the spiritual state is lacking, the inclination toward community exists in virtually every soul. It is simply part of the soil on which every community is founded.

And community itself is an anomaly. This is where theology enters in, and most important of all, our common striving for God.

Without this, community—or at least meaningful community—is impossible. For centuries, but especially in the past 200 years or so, countless utopian societies have sprung up in our world, particularly in idealistic and spiritually diverse North America. Most have become relics, because once they reached deep water, they did not possess a sufficient keel to center them.

There are those who say the Hutterites are shipwrecked as well. Despite a lack of aggressive outreach among the colonies, and an acknowledged need for deep spiritual renewal in many places, the Hutterian Church remains very much a living, changing group. Just comparing the colonies of today with the scholarship of even a few years ago will show a broad spectrum of changes and different attitudes brought on by a number of diverse influences, even though the basic mechanics of Hutterian life remain the same.

Granted, the majority of the 400 or so Hutterite colonies in North America would probably be unwilling, or at least very hesitant, about taking in newcomers, which places some very serious limits on the church as a whole. Still, among the communities themselves, there remains a distinct line of progression, a kind of momentum that seems to assure a future for every community and its daughter settlements. With or without converts, the communities fully expect to endure, and they very well could.

A concern I return to occasionally is one that afflicts most churches, but I think it is rather central to the Hutterites' lack of involvement in social causes and people's perceptions of us as backward or out of touch. I believe that after centuries of flight, and after decade upon decade of separation and apartness, we have lost our sorrow, our deep concern for the plight of others. We have replaced this sorrow with stoicism, but this is not enough. This is serious.

In the history of the Hutterites, we can see periods in which the emphasis on communalism had all but disappeared. These were also, without exception, times of great spiritual decline. No doubt, the Hutterites of those days were looked upon as a failed endeavor, if they were not forgotten or overlooked altogether. Having forsaken their earlier zeal for communalism, propelled as this was by persecution, the brothers went into a slow but numbing decline—a trend that was reversed, we are told, by nothing short of divine intervention.

The communal vision of Hutterite Michael Waldner, who restored community of goods in the mid-1800s in the Ukraine, was more than a biblical philosophical longing. To read the accounts he left, an actual vision from beyond left him convicted of the rightness of the communal path. On one side, he saw divine joy and salvation for those who shared all and lived together as one; on the other waited a blistering eternity of fire. One can imagine this hellish imagery, aside from appearing to be a visible, viable warning, represented also the inner despair some of the brothers and sisters must have been feeling, finding themselves in this state of decline. This fire was a trial and punishment of the present, not just of the future. By traveling back to the Christic, communal center of generations past, Waldner felt the Hutterites would find their only chance at rehabilitation and salvation. This they did, even though many abandoned the communities, and even more migrated to North America, only to strike out on their own once they had arrived.

But perhaps the Hutterites, more than any other group in modern times, show that without Christ-centeredness, without an unfailing emphasis on God over any man, community (and indeed true Christianity) is impossible.

True, other communities have existed that were not spiritual in foundation, but which pursued a certain ideal or lifestyle. This, too, is building on sand, because, invariably, differences of opinion arise. And when humans cannot solve these problems of day-to-day living, where can we turn? In spiritual communities, the answer is obvious; in those without such grounding, drift and eventually destruction are inevitable.

This does not mean, though, that Hutterites are immune to everything or that we will be here in another 100 years. It simply means that God has suffered us to survive, and that for now, anyway, we remain in his grace.

This is a mystery, to be certain, a mystery we will never be able to discern and which we should simply accept as it is.

This is what we believe.

Confessions of a Hutterite Convert

Robert Rhodes lives in the Starland Hutterite Colony in Gibbon, Minnesota.

The Decade's Knowledge and the Ancients' Wisdom

by Levi Miller

Se levantan sus hijos y la llaman dichosa.
— Proverbios 31:28

During this past winter my wife Gloria and a number of her college women friends met in Florida for a few days. Gloria told me that what these baby-boomer women discovered, perhaps somewhat to their surprise, is that they are all still married to their first husbands. Her friends are quite successful business and professional women, and I began to wonder how they missed their decade's knowledge.

I was an editor during the '70s when we were doing a number of religious books that tended to legitimize divorce; an alternate lifestyle, we called it. It was heady fresh air from what we called the oppressive '50s marriage culture, but I was skeptical whether the church should be so embracing of divorce and remarriage.

Now even social science in a tolerant culture is saying that monogamous marriage is healthier for kids; what common sense and biblical wisdom would have said all along.

But in the throes of romantic individual freedom released in the '60s, we encouraged parents to switch rather than fight. The church even sometimes adopted the culture's terms for the argument: restriction was monogamy and freedom was divorce. But on family issues, the Christian wisdom of the ages is generally better than the pop culture and social science knowledge of the decade. Popular code words depend on the point of view. Restriction for whom and freedom for whom?

I recently read a manuscript by a dozen elderly men who are trying to legitimize same-sex behavior, trying to Christianize it by having homosexuals and lesbians marry each other. Again, I find myself skeptical of their project.

It begins with trust—or lack of it. I have had some skepticism when elderly people who were brought up on one ethic too openly embrace another—especially one the Bible has called sin. They, after all, will not live with the consequences of their late-life conversions.

Some of the earliest apologists for divorce were elderly parents who claimed their adult children were suffering from the church's stigmatization of divorce. But it was really the innocent grandchildren who suffered the most and have to live longest with these decisions.

The neo-conservatives contributed a helpful insight in the '80s when they talked about unintended consequences of decisions and policies. It took several decades to discover the unintended consequences of liberal welfare laws and their effect on family life. Once the results rolled in, we revised our welfare policies in the mid '90s to reflect a more ancient wisdom that work is better than not working and two parents are better than one.

Making a legislative switch on biblical teaching is not as easy, however, as it is to reform national welfare legislation. For Christians, making these decisions has long-term consequences—and some unintended consequences—the quality of community life, definitions of family, and the credibility of the Scriptures.

Catholics have the papal office as a ballast in making these choices, and conservative Protestants have the Bible, but liberal Protestants are especially vulnerable to the popular opinion of the decade. To the extent that families and Christian communities take their insights from liberal Protestantism, they lose their ability to critique their culture on family norms and to provide a healthy and loving alternative.

All of which is to go back to Gloria's middle-aged college friends. Whether because of family, community, genes, Christian influence, biblical teaching, love, or some combination of any of these, they defied the odds of their generation and are once-married. On balance, their children and grandchildren can be thankful and are blessed. *Gloria, te amo.*

Levi Miller, Scottdale, Pennsylvania, is a writer and editor.

What I Can Do To Make Martin Luther King, Jr.'s Dream Come True

by Adira Paramitha Wijaya

Martin Luther King, Jr. envisioned the day when all people, regardless of their skin colors, could sit together at the table of brotherhood. If this dream should come true, I should make it mine also. Underlying this dream is a conviction that I should judge others on the basis of their inner qualities, not their outward appearances. I believe that by doing this I will make Martin Luther King, Jr.'s dream come true.

God has created every single human being in his own image. He has created everyone as equals, so why should skin color matter? I should not be a racist. I should not be afraid of shaking hands with people of different colors. Instead, I should be will-ing to care for people who are different from myself. Yes, we may have different appearances, but inside we're the same. I should be a person with a humble heart, someone who judges others by their souls, not by their skin colors, smartness, richness, or anything else.

I should not judge others the way many contem-poraries of Martin Luther King, Jr. did. They judged others as if they were judging a rose. They saw only the thorny stem of the rose, while ignoring its beautiful bud. That is why they were unable to see the beauty of the soul within a person. I should not be one of these people. If I want to make Martin Luther King, Jr.'s dream come true, I have to see others through the eyes of God.

This essay by Adira Wijaya, age 11, won first place in the elementary school division of the Martin Luther King, Jr. Essay Contest held citywide in Pasadena, California, January 2000. Adira and her Indonesian Mennonite family are currently living in Pasadena where her father is studying.

Common Tricks
of the River

by Paul Conrad

There is a magical moment in every river journey
when I realize I am no longer what I was. Perhaps it
happens because the sounds have all become liquid.
Maybe it happens because time and speed have
become bounded by the flow of the river. Perhaps it's
the concentrated awareness of immediate surround-
ings—the constant reading of the face of the water
and its banks for the best passage. Or perhaps it's the
light and shadow falling always in curves and circles,
unimpeded by the straight lines of architecture and
time. Or maybe it's the perpetual fishy smell, now
and again augmented by the cool downdraft off the
bluff, bringing with it the tang of hemlock and pine
and the traces of distant fire. It is a slow and exhilarating realization—I have become part of the ancient
and alternative world of the river.

It's a mystery. I asked several river enthusiasts why
they like the river so much. It was a wonderful way
to kill the conversation. There were mumbled and
almost apologetic references to solitude, relaxation,
and being in the midst of nature. But mostly silence.
One silence lasted two weeks. "I think," the ordinary,
wage-earning Menno finally reported, "that there are

three elemental things—earth, fire, and water. Being on the river brings forth a deep and primal response from the psyche. It's like staring at a fire and becoming mesmerized." Well, maybe.

So we river enthusiasts are an anecdotal bunch. We speak at length and with clarity of our experiences: beavers within paddle reach, deer on the banks, mystical sunrises and sunsets over the water, plumes of mist, blue herons and bald eagles, and dark and turbulent water. Our words wheel about the mystery of the river—just don't ask us to explain. You have to be there to understand. It's why we return time and again—to be tricked by the river.

We've been on the river just long enough to start thinking about food. The morning has been overcast and misty. No chance of showers, the weatherman said in a monotone; the overcast will burn off by noon. The river narrows here against a bluff two silos tall and gnaws beneath sandstone outcroppings. My 14-year-old boy wants to stop and fish. He's developed a fascination with small-mouth bass. We once fished for several hours without success. As we left, a nice one leaped into the canoe, scaring everyone. I think he's taken it personally.

We pull out on the gravel bar on the shallow side. Two things happen simultaneously; we hear the rumble of distant thunder, and a small bird skims across the river, erratically, just above the water. We are both watching it when the water boils and a fish launches itself at the bird.

It's over in a blink of the eye—the bird off in the trees and the water returning to black slickness. "Wow," says the boy with wide eyes.

Thunder again, closer, I'm sure, but the river bends around the corner and the hills block any long view. A few minutes of fishing, standing knee-deep in the water, feeling its constant push and I'm certain we're in for a soaking. The thunder has taken on an ominous continual mutter and it is definitely closer.

The boy and I carry the canoe up the river bank and through the brush. "The electrical charge from a lightning strike can carry a quarter mile up or down the water," I tell him as if I've verified this personally. It's the kind of thing fathers are supposed to say, I imagine. At least it's the kind of thing that interests him. It's suddenly dark and blasts of wind puncture the calm as we stash the canoe beyond the reach of the trees. A wall of white crests the far hill and sweeps toward us as we head into the nearby corn field.

We squat between the rows and are engulfed. Lightning flickers constantly with occasional brilliant flashes. The thunder crescendoes, recedes, crashes again. The ground shudders. We hear a roar as hail drives in fitful sheets.

The ground becomes covered with ice. Bursts of wind lean the cornstalks down to our shoulders, first one way and then another.

And it all gets louder and stronger and louder and stronger. Rain now, pelting down, puddling between the rows; lightning that sizzles and breaks into deafening claps of thunder before the glare fades. And everywhere the roar of the wind. I recall that John Muir once went through a thunderstorm lashed to a tree top. What a fool, I think, because this is getting to be scary stuff. I catch the boy's eye and give him the thumbs up (it's too loud to talk). I image it's the kind of thing fathers are supposed to do. He seems to be weathering the storm well—at least he's not flinching with each flash of lightning like I catch myself doing.

And it gets worse. I think unkind thoughts about weathermen. I start to ask myself ancient questions— questions I've been told are unnecessary and misdirected—questions that have probably been asked for centuries up and down this river: How appropriate is our presence here? Have I done anything that has annoyed cosmic powers? If so, what kind of aim do they have? Why didn't I actually read Kushner's book and take seriously this medicine man's counsel? These questions take on unseemly weight in the noon darkness in the world of the river.

The storm gradually passes. Finally there is simply a steady drizzle, brief gusts of wind, thunder beyond the far side of the valley. "The strongest lightning strikes occur on the back side of the storm," I say, because I've heard it's so. "Let's give it another 10 minutes."

As we wait, the boy says, "I've been wondering— that fish almost catching the bird is pretty amazing. The bird was moving, the water was moving, the fish was moving, and the fish was looking through water into air in order to time its jump. Do you think it came so close because it's done it a lot before, or does it somehow automatically know how to do it?"

He compares the incident to his hitting a baseball, decides the fish's leap is probably more difficult— more variables—reflects on the hours he's spent practicing his hitting, can't imagine a fish getting that much practice unless they have birdie batting cages, can't believe a fish would innately know how to gauge such a leap, decides it probably does, in large part, with some practice thrown in, and finally wonders what unimaginable process took place to give the fish such innate judgment, and wonders if humans might have similar processes imbedded in them.

I make intelligent grunting noises and declare it time to go. We've just stood when lightning flashes in a brilliant glare, thunder a solid wall that shudders the ground and rumbles into the distance. "Last strikes are strongest," I say when I can speak again.

Ah, the questions the river tricks us into asking.

My friend Pratt and I are on the second day of a long-anticipated three-day river journey. We are drifting on a slow current. Four hundred yards ahead, the river simply disappears into a rock wall. We're both confused as to which side we should take. Pratt has his topographical map spread across his knees. "It goes left. I'm positive. See how the hills bank to the left?"

I really can't tell. "It would be embarrassing to misplace a river 200 years wide. Left it is," I say. We dodge around snags and make our way slowly to the left. We enter a bank of mist, remnants of the morning fog, and promptly run out of river. We stare dumbly at one another. This is impossible. We have

maps, common sense, eyes in our heads. I feel the
certainty of perception disappear, and a dizzy vacuum
of imagination arises. What we know can't be that
wrong; what we see can't be right.

"We could follow the current," Pratt says reasonably.
"The current's running upstream, the direction that we
came from," I point out. "I'm getting spooked," says
Pratt. Our explanations aren't working. And it is getting
spooky. It's a common trick of the river.

Rivers delight in getting me lost. They take my perceptions of time and direction and distance and
scramble them into a dark and disorienting vortex.
This once caused me considerable distress. It is, well,
ah, stupid, to be lost on a river, sitting on tons of moving water that with certainty go from Point A to Point
B and to be so disoriented and without markers. I
start imagining that somehow around one of the
bends, I've taken a channel that has slipped me into
another universe.

The river that runs south also runs east, west, and
north at various times. Certainty of direction and
place are nice and necessary in daily life. They
become a hazard on the river. In a humbling way it's
good to be reminded that what we know is never
enough.

Pratt and I do follow the current. It does go
upstream. It's a huge eddy, made by the river's sharp
bend to the right.

The river narrows and picks up speed and turns
dark and roiling. Snags bob in the water. Upwellings
big as kitchens grab the canoe like invisible hands.
The channel splits, angles, curves. The wind sweeps

across the water, creating false riffles. And suddenly we stop. We simply stop. Or I think we do. Except it seems like we are racing upstream. The illusion is so real and comprehensive that I start to steer backwards, a bad thing to do with the front of the canoe lodging on a subterranean snag. The current catches the canoe and swings it broadside, tipping the downstream side dangerously near the water.

"Lean upstream," I yell to Pratt. He leans the wrong way.

"The other upstream," I yell.

The canoe rights itself. We are facing upstream. Except now the water races past us, and it appears we are moving upstream. We sit in the middle of the dark water and discuss the situation. We gradually dispel the illusions.

"If we get off this thing, I would like to land and see if the ground is solid," I say.

We do and it is, I think.

Rivers force me back in time. They have been gnawing their way into the earth here in north-central Ohio for over 12,000 years. The effort is read on the rocks and flood plains they have cut and created. The time and effort I spend building houses with a projected lifetime of 50 years become highly qualified. People have followed these same rivers for centuries. Paleo people lived on these bluffs. Indians lived here. White settlers followed them.

The stories abound. On one afternoon I hear five versions of the same story concerning white woman's rock—a white woman, pursued by Indians, jumped off the rock face into the swirling waters of the

Walhonding. I later found the story in a book of oral history. A report from the mid-1800s ended with the declarations that "the locals forever delight in telling this story to the visitor."

Mary Harris lived near these rivers. She is thought to be the first white person ever in this area. Captured in Pennsylvania as a young girl, she married the son of a prominent chief and considered native life vastly superior to white life. This lasted until her husband decided that if one white wife is good, two would be better. Mary Harris didn't like the idea or the second wife.

The details are murky but some remain—a tomahawked husband, an executed second wife and Mary Harris remarried.

On a hill nearby, Colonel Bouquet once camped with 1500 soldiers he had marched upstream from Pittsburgh. It was here that white captives were returned, with great sadness on the part of many, having come to consider this area home, and their captors family and friends. Some were married with children. And they all crossed this river.

And then there was the white settler from Loudonville who made a boat of rough sawed lumber. He loaded it with wheat and other farm products with the intention of floating downstream and selling everything at the first good market. The prices always seemed better downstream. He ended up in New Orleans, where he heard that the best prices were in Virginia. He shipped himself and the wheat there and walked home, arriving home two years after his departure.

I somehow understand the story. He was tricked by the river. It's what happens when the river journey ends. You stand by the river and peer downstream, reading the surface and imagining what happens beyond the next bend.

The river has been here long before and will be here long after. The native villages are gone. Only whispers of a few lives lived along the river remain. The homestead of the man who chased the horse thief all the way to Zanesville is gone. The Moravian settlement is gone. So too are many bridges—only towering abutments of cut sandstone remain. The river undercuts and topples the reinforcements we construct—wooden pilings lean across the water, concrete and sandstone walls topple. Even the person who built a wall of old refrigerators poured full of cement has had his efforts overcome by the river.

The rivers have silted our dams full. The old ones crack and buckle. We aren't all that much in the context of the river. Just brief visitors, as were the mastodons who drank from this water.

The river journey ends. The river is left behind. Daily life resumes. Directions reasonably align. Time and distance are contained, perceptions routine. It is then that the river plays its nastiest trick. The river sends visions of places visited and waters traveled. These recollections appear full-blown and overwhelming, and suddenly I am transported to another world, where the water flows endlessly and the smell of fish and the surrounding woods fills my head and return is essential.

Paul Conrad is a farmer/carpenter living in Holmes County, Ohio.

Whole . . . *and Single*

by Dawn J. Ranck

I bought my first house with my sister when I was
25. People constantly asked us, "What happens if one
of you marries?" My response was always, "At least
we'll have had a good investment!"

During the last several years, I have needed to confront the real possibility of lifelong singleness. A part
within me yearns deeply for a romantic, sexual relationship. Sometimes wishing for marriage consumes
me. I have asked God time and time again, "WHY?
WHY ME?" Why am I singled out?! Why does no one
choose me?!"

Naomi Levy, a Jewish rabbi, in her book To *Begin
Again: The Journey Toward Comfort, Strength, and Faith
in Difficult Times,* writes:

> There are questions that can never be answered
> properly with words. The answers are not matters
> of logic. Nor are they about philosophy or theolo-
> gy. Each one of us carries a question for which
> there is no answer . . . The question I have tried to
> answer again and again . . . is not: Why did this
> happen? But: How will I go on?[1]

Nearly half the American population is single. This
is a recent phenomenon. In the 1950s the American
family consisted of father, mother, children, dog, in a
house with a white picket fence. At least, this is what

our ideological memories tell us. The upheaval and
social revolution of the 1960s shattered this idyllic
image. The religious community especially was left
confused and frightened. Suddenly "family values"
was the focus. Many Christians feared the decaying
family, and soon all of society's ills were blamed on
the "breakdown of the family."

The Jewish world of the Old Testament viewed bar-
renness and lifelong singleness as curses. It was
through children, especially male children, that a person survived after death. Jesus taught that salvation
did not rely upon offspring; rather that salvation and
eternal life came through following him. Jesus created
a whole new family structure — the church. This new
family increased the value of the single person.
Scripture affirms that our sense of wholeness and
identity comes from our identity in Christ, not our
marital status.

It is difficult to argue against marriage and family,
but these were not the number one priorities of Jesus.
This "family theology" that churches emphasize is not
biblical theology. According to Albert Y. Hsu, "A truly
Christian view of both singleness and marriage will
honor both equally without disparaging one or the
other. Recovering such a balance is the first step
toward a church where singles are valued equally
with marrieds."[2]

Although nearly half of the adult population is single, yet only about 15% of the people in our churches
are single. Church is the place where my singleness is
most evident to me. In the working world and at
school, people come as individuals. Although they
may talk about their spouses and children, they and I

are both there on equal terms. On a Sunday morning, people come to church as families. They sit together, both parents caring for the children. While I see this as good on one hand, on the other it makes it hard to sit alone. I'm not recommending that we go back to men sitting on one side and women on the other, but I can't help wondering if singles would feel more included if we did.

One of my friends was a member of a church that decided to call their young adult Sunday School class "Pairs and Spares." She was the only "spare" and in a few weeks moved to a different church. Many churches need to have sensitivity training in regard to singles, in the same way as they train about racism and how to treat those who are otherwise marginalized.

We need to rediscover the concept of interrelatedness within the body of Christ. A couple of weeks ago the mother of a girl whom I mentor at church invited me to their house for an evening meal. As the family and I ate, talked, and laughed together, I was struck by how good it felt to be a part of a family. Although I don't often eat alone, I rarely eat with a family. I was struck by the gift that the family gave me, and wondered how I can help people gain an awareness of the interrelatedness of families and singles. Singles can come alongside parents and help with childcare. The family can embrace the single and provide a secondary home.

God created us as social beings. Being a Christian is not an individual journey. It is a group effort lived in community. The church is God's family on earth. God reminds us that we are part of a family far more significant and enduring than the biological family.

One in four households in America consists of a person living alone. I have learned to be self-reliant. I have also learned that it's okay to need other people. It's much easier to get a six-foot friend to put a new bulb in my porch light than to stand struggling by myself on a shaky porch swing. I've learned that rugged individualism leaves little room for others or for God.

"The task we have to face is the same, whether we are married or single: To live a fulfilled life in spite of many unfulfilled desires,"[3] wrote Walter Trobisch. One of my friends has given me a wonderful gift. There are times when her life is hard and she envies my singleness, and there are other times when I envy her married state. By sharing with each other, we each realize that neither marriage nor singleness is perfect.

When I think back over my life, I'm dismayed at the amount of time that I have spent worrying about relationships, or the lack thereof. I wish I had spent more time dwelling on the present and less time worrying about the future. "It is not wrong to hope for marriage or to recognize that marriage is a possibility for the future," Gary Collins says, "but it is not healthy to build our lives around events that are uncertain. Instead, individuals, especially Christians, must learn both to prepare for the future and to live fully in the present."[4] I am realizing that I can't always change my circumstances, but I can choose my attitude toward being single, as well as how I live my life as a single.

There are things in life that are far more important than whether or not I will marry. It's difficult, but I

recognize that I need to hand my life over to God—
all my dreams, hopes, and desires for a spouse. I am
called to live my life fully for Christ regardless of my
marital status. I want to be able to say with Paul, ". . .
I have learned to be content with whatever I have . . .
in any and all circumstances. I can do all things
through him who strengthens me" (Philippians 4:11-
13). To serve God whatever the circumstances—that is
God's will for me.

1 Naomi Levy, *To Begin Again: The Journey Toward Comfort, Strength, and Faith in Difficult Times* (New York, NY: Ballantine Books, 1998), p 8.

2 Albert Y. Hsu, *Singles at the Crossroads: A Fresh Perspective on Christian Singleness* (Downers Grove, IL: Intervarsity Press, 1997), p 45.

3 Walter Trobisch, *Love Is a Feeling to Be Learned* (Downers Grove, IL: Intervarsity Press, 1971), p 18.

4 Gary Collins, as quoted in Hsu, p. 109.

*Dawn Ranch is a 35-year-old single student at Eastern
Mennonite Seminary, where she is enrolled in a Masters
of Divinity program.*

The Confession of a Pack Rat

by Gerald Studer

I confess to having the acquisitive instincts of a
pack rat. A major expression of this is that I have
assembled a Bible collection within the last 53 years
that now numbers well over 5,000 volumes, including
more than 800 different languages.

Evan Esar once said that "people who have hobbies
seldom go crazy, but those who have to live with
them do." I trust that the first part of this statement
shall continue to prove accurate, but I must differ
with the conclusion. While my wife, Marilyn, is not
inclined as I am, she has proven to be a companion
tolerant of my penchant for Bibles through our more
than 50 years together.

I can say in self-defense that she knew of my hobby
before marrying me. We have worked out a satisfactory
agreement—I shall use no family income to enhance the
collection, and furthermore, I shall give all those books
a good dusting once a year, whether they need it or not.
I frankly suspect that she, too, has enjoyed the collection much of the time, though the books do occupy a
considerable amount of space.

I learned in my teens that with my modest income I
would have to make some tough choices. As Bulwer-
Lytton once said of hobbies, "It will not do to have
more than one at a time," so I made the calculated decision in my teens to sell my small stamp collection in

order to concentrate on Bibles. Actually, I made the decision to begin accumulating versions of the English Bible when I discovered early on in my preparation for the ministry that different renderings of the same verse or passage frequently shed light upon its meaning. Only when my pursuit began "growing like Topsy" did I discover that I was, in truth, developing a collection.

Most of the time the collection has grown slowly by the addition of a volume here and another there, garnered from used book shops, Provident Bookstore, book review services, articles and advertisements, publications I receive, Bible-collecting friends, or just other friends who happened to have or know of an item that I could obtain. I have rummaged through such sources both here in the States and abroad, so that by now the word has gotten around and I find people writing to me of items they have learned of that I might be interested in.

For some years, I made an annual trip to a Bible Society headquarters located only two hours away from our home in Lansdale, Pennsylvania, to look through their discard closet before they called the trash man to haul the miscellaneous collection away. This effort always rewarded me with a box or two of desirable items.

Then the day came when the librarian, who was my contact at the Society, was about to retire. I discovered on my next visit that the librarian had gone through a vast backlog of material before leaving her post and had left a truckload of 40 large boxes of duplicates. Realizing that examining such a huge number of boxes might have taken me a week, I returned home empty-handed and proposed to a neighbor/

church member that we make the trip with his panel truck. He readily agreed.

It took me a year and a half of spare evenings to go through this windfall of books, but I was richly repaid when I discovered what a treasure trove it was! Prior to this I had not gone very far into foreign language Bibles, but now my collection suddenly made a jump from a mere handful to well over 800 different languages—nearly half of the total number of languages into which a book, or testament, or the entire Bible, had been translated.

While I read only English fluently and have only a minimal acquaintance with Latin, Greek, Hebrew, and German, yet the research which I have done with regard to many of these volumes has been an exciting voyage of discovery and inspiration. I have treasured the many opportunities I have had to share a bit of this excitement with groups of various kinds that I have been invited to address.

My wife reminds me from time to time that the truck that moved us from my former pastorate at Scottdale, Pennsylvania, to my most recent one at Lansdale, Pennsylvania, was half-full of books. To this charge I can only plead guilty as charged with a deep sense of satisfaction! But even before we came to Lansdale in 1973, we knew that something would have to be done, for the collection was crowding our household. So we prepared a proposal which we sent to various Mennonite colleges regarding our donating the collection. The decision was eventually made in 1970 to donate the entire collection to my alma mater, Associated Mennonite Biblical Seminary in Elkhart, Indiana.

Consequently, each year as few as two cartons or as many as eight are delivered to the library there, and with each delivery the growing collection is gradually transferred from our home to its ultimate destination. This has gone on for 30 years, so that now the library has over 400 shelf-feet filled and a sizable number more still to come. A substantial portion of the collection is on permanent display in glass-doored cabinets where the books are available for use by students and researchers. Already more than two-thirds of the total collection has been delivered, and the library will receive the balance of the collection in due time.

I send annually only those I feel I can most readily do without, which means that the most fascinating and, in some cases, the most valuable, volumes will be added last. By such a process, I have kept a representative collection for public displays and am able to maintain some open space for new accessions. On my retirement income, these accessions consist largely of new translations and related books that I receive for review in our quarterly publication.

Like a tree, the collection has branched out in many directions. As a collector, I admit to an inability to limit the collection to only certain narrow boundaries. Consequently, the collection has the following subsections:

1) The English Bible in its various versions and editions, both as a complete Bible or as a part—one of the Testaments, for example; or a portion of one, such as the Old Testament poetic books; or even a single book;

2) Non-English Bibles;

3) Abridged Bibles;

4) Bible story books;

5) Illustrated Bibles—visual "translations" that go all the way from children's Bible story books to the illuminated calligraphy of the Middle Ages and the symbolic depictions of modern times;

6) Books about the Bible, including histories of the Bible in a given or various languages, missionary uses, histories of translations, printings, distribution, etc.;

7) Summaries and concordances;

8) Rare pages and replicas;

9) Miscellaneous related items, such as the Thomason Medallic Bible, the large picture of Christ made solely by variations in the penmanship and spacing of words, the Lord's Prayer on a single piece of typeface, etc.; and finally,

10) Miniatures.

Obviously, I am a generalist!

Among these categories are Bibles that have particular interest to Mennonites, beginning with the pre-Lutheran Froschauer Bible of 1571, or the Rodolphe Petter translation of the Bible in the Cheyenne Indian language, or the Trique New Testament and abridged Old Testament of the Mexican Indian tribe, done by a Mennonite missionary with the help of a partially paralyzed Trique woman named Cecelia. Then there are the several Hutterite reprints of old German editions, the Daniel Kauffman Bible, and the Hindi-language Bible belonging to a Mennonite missionary.

Related to these are three German language Bibles printed by the Brethren printer Christopher Sauer (or Sower) in Germantown, Pennsylvania, or a Quaker English Bible of 1608 which is a pre-King James

Geneva version that has all the instances of God "swearing" stricken out and "affirmed" written in the margin, and portions of the Bible in Pennsylvania Dutch, Frisian, and Plautdietsch or Low German.

There is a beautiful 1538 Vulgate Bible bound in vellum and printed in Venice in the collection; a 1593 copy of the "earliest Latin Bible printed in England"; a copy of the first Bible (German) printed west of the Allgehenies in 1814, which was once the pulpit Bible of a Mennonite congregation in Ohio; a 1765 Nurnberg Bible with its many magnificent full-page pictures of German rulers; the 1613 folio King James Version which is a comedy of typographical errors; a handwritten book of Psalms on 166 leaves of animal skin in the ancient Gheez language of the Coptic Church; the 1876 Julia Smith Bible of Hartford, Connecticut; a Gospel of Mark in Mongolian, read perpendicularly and printed in 1832; a miniature New Testament printed in 1844 with two handpainted scenes of an English skyline on the fore-edges of the pages; a first-edition copy of the first book published by the British and Foreign Bible Society in 1804, and a copy of the Gospel of John in the Mohawk Indian language.

One could go on and on to mention other curiosities of various kinds, including the entire Bible, page-for-page on a single 2 x 2 inch slide, or a bound Bible (portion) the size of an aspirin, or an even smaller complete New Testament in a plastic case to be worn as a necklace, or a New Testament corrected by spirits, and so on and so on.

It is doubtful whether any book other than the Bible has been subjected to so many and such esoteric adaptations. But the Bible's purpose to be the instrument of salvation to all humankind everywhere must never be lost sight of. I was awestruck when in accessioning several foreign language Bibles, I came across the book of Matthew in the South Seas island Binumarien language, only to learn that while missionaries spent many years mastering this language and reducing it to writing, there are only 143 people in all the world who speak the language. And there was the puzzling moment when I accessioned a complete Bible in the Faroese language, only to discover when searching a world map for its location, that it is an island of Europe.

The collection has provided endless hours of fascination and information for me. I desire that it provide the same for a host of others who can benefit from its presence in the library of the Associated Mennonite Biblical Seminary in Elkhart, Indiana.

Gerald Studer is a longtime pastor living in Lansdale, Pennsylvania.

The Answer is YES!

by Charles Christano

I love the song "There Is a Balm in Gilead," especially when my heart is hurting so deeply because of
the many atrocities, violence, and injustices done
around us. Millions of people are refugees worldwide,
even in their own countries. In our own land, the
String of Pearls in the Indonesian Archipelago—the
Land of Hospitality and Harmony—in no time, our
country has become so chaotic and turbulent!

In the midst of various world religions for more
than three decades, and after the demise of the
Indonesian Communist Party, we enjoyed peaceful
coexistence, stability, rapid development, and prosper-
ity. In fact, so much was going well that not a few
world economists named us one of the miracles of the
Two-Thirds World countries, the "upcoming tiger" in
Asia. But all of that was nothing but a house of cards.

Freedom in the hands of the immature and inexperi-
enced is a nightmare. The elites deliver great rhetoric
which vaporizes like thin air. The streets become stages
for new emerging heroes. And they bring along many
supporters who turn the streets into killing fields.
Hundreds are killed; many more are injured.

Pent-up dissatisfaction and frustrations from living
under repressive governments explode. Like a stam-

pede, various groups rush in to get their long awaited dreams. The spirit of revenge is rampant. Law enforcement is impotent.

CCN (collusion, corruption, and nepotism) is the name of the game. What happened during the earlier government is being repeated at a higher speed everywhere. The people's justice is much talked about these days. Meanwhile, over a million of our people have become refugees.

Ethnic cleansing, though being denied, takes place on several islands. Our banking system is wobbling. Our currency has become nearly worthless. Unemployment is growing, and millions of students can no longer continue their schooling. At least one generation is being lost. Another one is undernourished. Our future is so bleak.

We have been praying for many months. Rallies are organized to encourage thousands of different religious adherents to pray together.

Floods, earthquakes, and landslides have claimed unnumbered lives. Famine has caused jobless youngsters to turn to robberies, lootings, killings, even gang fights. Drug dealers are prospering in the middle of such multifaceted sufferings.

I have no words to respond when I am asked, "Is there a God?" "Does God really care?" "Where is He and what is He doing when we are hurting?" "What is the point of having a religion if religious leaders cannot live up to what they teach?" Some even ask, "Isn't it better to live under a repressive government after all?"

My wife, Lisa, and I travel to many areas where lots of church buildings were destroyed, some pastors and church leaders martyred, and hundreds others have been forced to denounce Christ and embrace Islam. We who believe in nonviolence and try hard to be peacemakers, we are flabbergasted. I must admit that as we rode speedboats in order to avoid a land ambush, my heart was trembling with fear.

When I am challenged about my theological stance, I often have to admit that deep down in my heart, I don't know what I'd do if I had to face the same situation as those people I am visiting. I know that I often fail and disappoint Christ, the Prince of Peace. I am often hesitant to go to areas where the enmity is thick and bitter. Many lives have been wasted, spurred by anger and vengeance.

I remember Job so often when things get harder. Job was blameless and upright, a man who feared God and shunned evil (Job 1:8). But even Job had limits. One time he spewed out his deep frustration: "I loathe my very life; therefore I will give free reign to my complaint and speak out in the bitterness of my soul. I will say to God: Do not condemn me, but tell me what charges you have against me. Does it please you to oppress me, to spurn the work of your hands, while you smile on the scheme of the wicked? Do you have eyes of flesh? Do you see as a mortal sees?" (Job 10:1-4).

I am afraid that I can easily become just like Job's friends who unconsciously committed greater mistakes as they tried to comfort him during his distress. I often wonder and waver about offering any answers to those who are at the end of their ropes.

Is there a balm in Gilead? I believe there is. Job has gone before us, and so have many others since Job.

The writer of Hebrews recorded: "All these people were still living by faith when they died. They did not receive the things promised; they only saw them and welcomed them from a distance. And they admitted that they were aliens and strangers on earth" (Hebrews 11:13).

We'll never know how long Job had to wait to get God's answer to his challenge. We only know that his faith was kept by God, and in due time he was compensated with more than he had to begin (Job 42:12). But then, not everyone has the same wonderful experiences as Job had. Take us, and so many others around the world. We are still living, yes. Of course we have heard and read the wonderful promises. But sometimes we are tempted to think that God might lie or forget His promises.

I am of the opinion that God is never caught by surprise. He knows the end from the beginning. He knows who we are. "He knows how we are formed, he remembers that we are dust" (Psalm 103:14). But yet, not only am I tempted to get angry with God, I also often complain to Him. I am surprised with what I say to Him when I am in hot water. But then I know that God is not surprised at all.

Job asked God whether He has eyes of flesh, whether He sees as a mortal sees. By faith I believe that He does. Emmanuel, God with us—that is God's answer to Job and to everyone who has suffered and is now suffering unjustly. I have learned, but I am still learning again and again. Sometimes I succeed in believing, but I often fail, too. When things get rough and almost intolerable, I am reminded of Paul's admonition, "Your attitude should be the same as that of

Christ Jesus: Who being in the very nature God, did not consider equality with God something to be grasped, but made himself nothing, taking the very nature of a servant, being made in human likeness. And being found in appearance as a man, he humbled himself and became obedient to death—even death on a cross" (Philippians 2:5-8).

Once again I have to admit that I have not known everything. But by faith I want to learn to be faithful and obedient until that day when God leads me home. Sure, He answered Job during his time, but many others of the faithful died without receiving what they were promised.

I do not know what is going to happen. Come what may, I do know that God answered the very challenge that Job spewed out a long time ago. Although we are living long after Jesus became man, Jesus still lives. And He is living within us.

I guess each and every one of us just needs His grace. When worse becomes worst, Christ's grace is all that we need. And His grace is never overspent. So let us face the future with the knowledge that "He who began a good work in us will carry it on to completion, until the day of Christ Jesus" (Philippians 1:6). Amen.

Charles Christano is a pastor and leader in Kudus, Indonesia, and a past president of Mennonite World Conference.

A Word for Ethnic Churches

by Richard Showalter

Multi-culturalism is in. Diversity is a mantra. Globalization is a code word for the 21st century.

In contrast, the Greek root *ethno-* seems now to appear most often in phrases like "ethnic pride," "ethnic violence," and "ethnic hatred." The Cold War has passed into history, and in its place is an almost universal bewildering maze of ethnic tensions which rip apart the veneer of civility in societies everywhere. The Tutus and Hutus, the Irish and English, Serbs and Croats, Palestinian Arabs and Israeli Jews, European-Americans and African-Americans, and on and on.

Yet our ethnicity is a good gift from God. Every nuclear or extended family is a new beginning of ethnicity. (Families become clans, and clans become ethnic groups.) Every person born into the world becomes part of an ethnic group, with language, customs, and culture different from the majority of all other people.

Cultures emerge and disappear, but culture does not. As old ones die, new ones are formed.

All of us are in some sense prisoners of our cultures. With great effort, a few of us learn more than a half-dozen languages. A tiny circle in each generation learns 20 or 30, but human lifetimes are not long enough to go much further, even for the most brilliant.

Christian congregations are not unlike individuals. Each has its own corporate culture, and each tends to reflect quite accurately one of the thousands of human ethnic groups. A few, of course, may learn five or 10 "languages," and these are called multi-cultural churches. But many more are mono-cultural, reflecting one ethnic group.

It is time to accept and celebrate reality. Mono-cultural, ethnic congregations are okay. They are even beautiful, as African-Americans began to teach us in the 1960s.

To be specific, Swiss-German American and Dutch-Russian American traditional Mennonite congregations are ethnic churches. Are they therefore bad?

No. They are only bad if loyalty to their particular form of ethnicity is elevated above loyalty to Jesus as Lord. That's idolatry, ethnic idolatry.

On the other hand, replacing mono-culturalism with multi-culturalism does not automatically make a church better. In fact, it sometimes makes it worse. It is harder for leadership to be representative, for members to be understood, for unity to be achieved. Not impossible, just harder.

Of course, there are beautiful multi-cultural churches. May their tribes increase. And there are beautiful mono-cultural churches. May their tribe increase.

But at the end of the conversation, we would have to reckon that the vast majority of Christian churches since Pentecost have been what we would call ethnic churches, mono-cultural churches. The critical issue is not, were they ethnic? Rather, it is, were they faithful?

Jesus, after all, was "ethnic." As are we. All of us. Let's celebrate every ethnic form in which we come. Ethnicity is God's good gift. Then even more, let's celebrate our oneness in Christ, God's greatest gift.

Richard Showalter, Salunga, Pennsylvania, is president of Eastern Mennonite Missions.

Parables of the Kingdom and Other Faiths
How should Christians relate to people of other religions, or of no religion?
by Alain Epp Weaver

On the first Sunday of every month, a motley group of 20 to 30 people gathers on a windswept vacant lot in the middle of the Stateway Gardens housing project on Chicago's South Side. Members of the Vigil Against Violence, these people come together to remember those who have been killed on the South Side during the past year. Several banners bear the thousands of names of those who have died since 1994.

A community leader speaks for a few minutes on her opposition to violence. Though many of those who attend the vigil are active, committed Christians, the vigil itself doesn't have an exclusively Christian flavor. Jews, Muslims, and avowedly secular people also attend to form a community of resistance to violence and hope in a better future, a sign of God's peaceable kingdom.

The Vigil Against Violence is but one example of activities that bring faithful Christians into partnership with non-Christians. As North America becomes increasingly diverse religiously, the number of such interfaith coalitions will also grow. Partnerships with non-Christians are also commonplace in the church's relief and development work. In Lebanon, Jordan, and Palestine, for example, Mennonite Central Committee enters into arrangements with Muslim groups to promote peacebuilding efforts and bring aid to the needy.

Working with people of other faiths is simply an unavoidable condition of the church's mission in a multi-faith globe. Working side by side with non-Christians, however, can be an uncomfortable experience. In the course of the give and take of daily dialogue, Christians can be challenged by the words and deeds of non-Christian friends and colleagues. Mennonites working in Islamic contexts, for example, have seen God's Spirit at work among Muslims as they fast spiritually and physically during their holy month of Ramadan and as they witness to God's sovereignty over all of creation and history.

How are we to understand theologically the experience of receiving truth from non-Christians? One popular answer is that of the pluralist: There are many, equally valid paths to God. If the pluralist is correct, then explaining the reception of truth from non-Christians becomes a straightforward affair. But the pluralist option is problematic, at least for most Christians, because it involves a devaluation of traditional Christian claims about Jesus Christ. The vast majority of Christians throughout history have proclaimed Jesus Christ as the exclusive and final revelation of God. Pluralists, in contrast, proclaim that God is revealed not only in Jesus Christ but also outside of him.

Sectarian isolation

To give up claims about the exclusivity and finality of God's self-revelation in Jesus Christ will seem to most Christians too high a price to pay for explaining how we hear what we take to be God's truth from non-Christians. Much contemporary debate on inter-religious matters thus seems to leave traditional Christians in a bind: Either one affirms a plurality of revelations, of which Jesus Christ is but one example, or one proclaims Jesus Christ as the one true Word of God and retreats into sectarian isolation, denying in advance that non-Christians might speak true words.

But is this forced option genuine? Might there not be another way of approaching the question, one that would allow Christians to proclaim the exclusive character of God's revelation in Jesus Christ while also being open to the witness of non-Christians? I suggest we look to the writings of Karl Barth, the great Swiss theologian, for a helpful alternative. Barth's conception of true human words as "parables of the king-dom" points toward a stance that both proclaims the exclusiveness of God's self-revelation in Jesus Christ and is open to new truth from non-Christians (see Barth's *Church Dogmatics,* Vol. IV).

Fundamental for Barth is the premise that no human words or actions by themselves say what God says in Jesus Christ: Not the Bible, not church preaching and teaching, not the words of non-Christians. Jesus Christ, God's one true Word, stands above all human language and relativizes it. The truth of the Bible and church proclamation is based solely on God's free, electing grace in Jesus Christ, not on their character as human words. They are true to the extent that they are spoken by Jesus Christ as parables of his kingdom.

We Christians have heard God's Word in Scripture and the church's worship. On what theological grounds might we expect to hear it spoken outside of church walls? Our answer returns to Christology. Pluralists tend to have a low Christology: Jesus, for them, is but one prophet among others, *one* word of God rather than *the* Word of God. What, in contrast, would a high Christology mean for the question of truth in other religions? One answer would say that Jesus Christ is God's one true Word, and that, therefore, all religious words that do not bear his name are false. This answer, however, does not take Christ seriously enough. By denying that true words about God may be spoken by non-Christians, it restricts Christ's lordship to the church.

Witnesses to God's kingdom

Barth, in contrast, argues that because Christ's lordship extends over all of human history and creation, Christians should expect to hear true words about God spoken by non-Christians. These non-Christian words do not stand alongside Jesus Christ as alternative revelations of God, but stand within his lordship: They are spoken by him as parables of his kingdom. Even though non-Christians do not acknowledge Christ's lordship, they are still subject to it and can be made witnesses to God's kingdom. The true words they speak and the deeds they perform stand within God's Word in Christ rather than outside of him.

All well and good, one may say, but how do we know whether or not the words and actions of non-

Christians are parables of the kingdom? We can't
answer this question in advance of concrete dialogue,
says Barth; to set up supposedly foolproof criteria for
discerning what non-Christian words are true parables
of God's kingdom is to try to control the movement of
God's free, electing grace. We can ask if the word or
deed in question harmonizes with Scripture. We can
look to see how it fits the whole of church teaching.
We can examine what practical fruits the non-
Christian word brings forth in the lives of non-
Christians.

True parables will always lead Christians back into
Scripture, but sometimes this will mean that
Christians will have to give up their preconceptions
about what Scripture says. True parables will sometimes harmonize with church teaching, but at other
times the witness of true parables may call the church
to re-examine what it teaches. Above all, the Christian
must ask whether or not the words and deeds of non-
Christians point to Christ. Of course, we Christians
must ask the same question of our own words and
deeds.

The receptivity to God's word from outside the
church's walls demanded by Barth's parables of the
kingdom squares well with the traditional Mennonite
emphasis on nonresistance. Christians must forsake a
prideful insistence that God's word is spoken only
through us, not through others; we must abandon our
resistance to hearing that word spoken by non-
Christians.

In Christ, God has judged all human talk about the
divine and found it wanting; through Christ, God has
elected our words to proclaim the kingdom. Our gra-

cious election by God should prompt in us humility rather than triumphalism, should make us attentive to signs of God's grace outside the church's walls. In humility, then, we must enter into dialogue with people of other faiths, prepared not only to give witness to Christ but to receive a witness to Christ and his kingdom from those with whom we converse. Overseas workers with Mennonite Central Committee and Mennonite mission boards, as well as North American Mennonites living in interfaith environments, are engaged in such nonresistant dialogue. May all of us, as Mennonite Christians, pledge to be nonresistantly open to God's free word as we interact with our neighbors and co-workers of other faiths.

Alain Epp Weaver, Jerusalem, and his wife, Sonia, direct Mennonite Central Committee's program in Palestine.

A Sermon

The Virgin and the Unicorn

by Margaret Loewen Reimer

In this pre-Advent season, I thought it might be
appropriate to meditate on the Virgin and the unicorn. It was a popular subject in medieval art where
you often see the Virgin Mary pictured with a unicorn in an enclosed garden. What does it mean?

The scene has its roots, of course, in the legend of
the unicorn—that mythic creature usually pictured as
a white horse with a single horn. According to legend, the unicorn could be subdued and captured
only by a virgin. The unicorn thus became a symbol
of purity and female chastity. In Christian art, the
unicorn was associated with Mary's purity and the
scene became an allegory of the Annunciation.
Sometimes the unicorn was even associated with
Christ.

The enclosed or walled garden brings to mind the
garden of Paradise, but it also points to Mary's vir-
ginity (the enclosed womb). The idea comes from
Song of Solomon 4:12: "A garden enclosed is my sister, my spouse; a spring shut up, a fountain sealed."

I recall this scene for two reasons: 1) It illustrates
the imaginative riches of the biblical tradition, about
which I want to say a few words, and 2) it expresses
the interplay in the Christian tradition between the
sacred and the profane, between biblical faith and
cultural truth.

My interests have always focused on the point
where theology and literature intersect, where the
imagination of the Bible interacts with the so-called
"secular" imagination. That's uncomfortable territory
for some people, I've noticed. A few years ago, I
wrote an Advent reflection in the *Canadian Mennonite*
on the incarnation, using the apocryphal gospels of
Pseudo-Matthew and The Gospel of Thomas. These
books, just outside the boundaries of the biblical
canon, provide some fascinating variations on Jesus'
nativity and childhood, and I thought they might shed
some light on the version we are familiar with.

Some of our readers were quite alarmed and I had
a few intense phone calls about that article. I sensed a
kind of fear about venturing outside the protective
walls we have built around our Scriptures. We don't
like "outsiders" to tamper with our version of the
script. When Canadian Mennonite Bible College performed "Jesus Christ Superstar" two years ago, they
had to mount a major campaign to rationalize their
choice of a rock musical to the constituency. What we
do in those situations, of course, is try to sanctify the
event by emphasizing its orthodoxy, instead of celebrating its creativity. But we don't have to look outside the Bible to see how we try to protect our faith.
We're even afraid to look at some of the imaginative
stuff right in the Bible itself!

William Blake, the mystical English poet and artist,
said the Bible is the most entertaining book in the
world because it appeals first and foremost to the
imagination. We don't believe that, do we? Do we ever
read the Bible for entertainment or for fun? It strikes
me that we spend a lot of energy trying to stifle or

explain away the wild and wonderful elements of the
biblical imagination, to make it safe for moral instruc-
tion and religious piety. So we shy away from all those
horrible biblical stories of murder and incest and adultery, and then go and watch Melrose Place. We are
uncomfortable with the Bible's interest in angels and
demons and magical tricks, but we seem to enjoy The
X-Files and Buffy the Vampire Slayer. And how about
Star Wars? We gingerly try to "explain" John's version
in Revelation in terms we would never apply to
George Lucas's version. Why is that?

Well, an obvious reason is that we want to keep the
Bible sacred, to safeguard it for our faith. We want to
keep it clean and historical and useful. But we rob
ourselves of its rich imagination when we lock it
away in a religious closet, away from conversation
with the other art forms that inspire us every day.
Another reason for our difficulty is that the Bible is
simply too "foreign" and too overwhelming to accept
on its own terms. So we try to translate the Bible's
artistry into the language of piety or reason; we try to
reduce its many dimensions of reality into manage-
able meaning. (Biblical criticism has to take some of
the blame here—it has often helped to literalize that
which was literary.) I'm not just talking about reading
the Bible as narrative or story—we've done that one
to death. I'm talking about being open to the Bible's
other realms of reality, entering into the imagination
of the ancients.

In a lot of ways, we have the same difficulty with
the Bible's artistry that we have with contemporary
art. We don't know how to make sense of it or how to
hold all the clashing images together. It's hard to pack-

age in a coherent container. While our modernist obsession with empirical explanation has faded somewhat, we're not doing much better with understanding mystery or metaphor or contradiction. Maybe the Bible is closer to our post-modern imagination than we think. Maybe we need to let it speak more to us about fragmentation and non-linear reality, and how to gather disparate realities together in a meaningful whole.

My doctoral thesis in English literature had to do with the influence of the Old Testament imagination on English writers. During my thesis defense, my examiners became most agitated over my assumption of coherence. How could I assume a connection between the biblical worldview and the views of nineteenth century British writers? they asked. In a literary climate enamored of disjunction and discontinuity, it was difficult to communicate.

But that's the problem we all face today. How can we presume connections between the ancient worlds of the Bible and our world of television and the Internet, for example? Well, maybe we've got to let those worlds interact more with each other, especially in shaping the minds of our children. We do that when we tell our children Bible stories alongside other stories. It's not that big a leap, after all, from Samson to The Terminator, or from Tamar to the latest victim of incest in the news. Our teenagers know girls like Tamar—they are familiar with violence and despair and death in ways that we may not have been. Maybe those grim and uncomfortable parts of reality are what the Psalmist had in mind when he said, "I will utter dark sayings from of old [riddles of old things, says another version], things that we have heard and known, that our fathers have told us. We will not hide them from their children, but tell them to the coming generation."

As Christians, we believe that there is a continuity through the ages, that our stories are somehow linked to the biblical stories and to the history of the world. If we believe that, then we must also believe that biblical truths are related to other truths, that the Bible, in fact, is part of a much larger canon that includes the many cultural "texts" that shape us every day. We seem to be more interested in confining the Bible to an *intra-textual* debate—a debate within itself—than in opening it up to an *inter-textual* dialogue with the culture around us. That larger interplay, spurred by the imagination, is what shapes a larger faith.

Dorothy Sayers, British classics scholar and detective novelist, said that the seminal moment of her growing up was the moment she discovered that Ahasuerus from the Bible was the same person as Xerxes from history. Worlds suddenly came together. When my three children were still at home, we had a sort of "Family Summa"—our compendium of essential knowledge—hanging above our kitchen table. On it, the Nine Orders of Angels were listed beside the Nine Muses; the Seven Virtues beside the Seven Deadly Sins. The Olympic Pantheon was followed by the Twelve Tribes of Israel (not quite parallel). It was quirky but perhaps a nudge to the integrating powers of the imagination. Now lest you think all this is just some pet project of mine, I can claim inspiration from Mennonite history.

Quite recently, my father told me a startling story about my great-grandfather, a story I don't remember ever hearing before. I grew up in southern Manitoba in the heart of the Bergthaler Mennonite community. My great-grandparents had left Russia in 1874 to settle on the Canadian prairies. I know nothing about those ancestors of mine; we have no stories about their lives or thoughts, although I have their stern portraits hanging in the stairwell of my home. I have always imagined them to be uneducated, rigidly conservative, and too busy surviving to have time to think about anything.

So I was surprised when my father told me that Great-grandfather Rempel had told him one story about coming over on the boat from Russia. This is the only story I have from that generation. Great-grandpa Rempel said that all the way to Canada their ship was followed by mermaids—beautiful, golden-haired mermaids—and the children threw out pieces of bread to feed them. That's my family story from Mennonite history and I find it very inspiring. I wish that more of those stories were part of the Mennonite canon.

So back to the unicorns. You can find them in the Bible, you know. They appear at least seven times in the pages of the King James Version, having crept in by way of the Vulgate. Unhappily, later versions dropped the mysterious creatures in favour of banal historicity and we hear no more about unicorns. What a pity.

Scripture texts:

Psalm 78: 1-4: "I will open my mouth in a parable; I will utter dark sayings from of old, things that we have heard and known, that our fathers have told us. We will not hide them from their children, but tell to the coming generation the glorious deeds of the Lord, and his might, and the wonders which he has wrought."

Isaiah 45: "I will go before you and level the mountains, I will break in pieces the doors of bronze and cut asunder the bars of iron, I will give you the treasures of darkness and the hoards in secret places, that you may know that it is I, the Lord, the God of Israel, who call you by your name" (RSV).

(Unicorns in KJV: Numbers 23:22; Deuteronomy 33:17; Job 39:9,10; Psalm 29:6, 22:21, 92:10; Isaiah 34:7)

Margaret Loewen Reimer, Waterloo, Ontario, is associate editor of Canadian Mennonite.

Humor

Plain Dissy

by Merle Good

Martha-
Jane: Hey, there, Chakie, do ya haff a minute?

Jake: Vy shurah, Martha Chain. Vat's up?

M.J.   Vell, I don't quite know vonct, but that there Sunday School discussion hat me a bit fer-hoodult.

Jake: Ya don't sayah.

M.J.:   I'm twoah dumb, proply.

Jake: Can't quarrel vith ya there, Martha Chain!

M.J.:   Nowah, Chakie. It's chust that I can't ficker aut this consensus stuff. Can youah?

Jake: It's a bit ticklish, I bleef.

M.J.:   More than a bit. I thought vee vur tryin to ficker aut whoah shoult teach our class.

Jake: I bleef that's the drift, Martha Chain.

M.J.:   So vy can't vee chust wote?

Jake: That's the sixty-four huntrit dollar question, ain't it?

M.J.:   Thousant.

Jake: Vat?

M.J.:   Sixty-four thousant. Vy, Chakie, are ya confused? It vas the sixty-four *thousant* dollar question, don't ya remember still? Ohah, I bet ya didn't see any tee wee back thenadays, did ya nowah, Chakie?

Jake: I hartlee see none nowah.

M.J.: Vat in the vurlt vas vee talking abaut, any howah? I know I'm all steamt up inside, but I'm afrait I'm forgettin vy.

Jake: Consensus.

M.J.: Oh, consensus! Oh, it makes vun mad! I shoult hasten to say I don't think it's right to be mad at church, Chakie, but I can't quite help it, bleef me. I mean, chust to decite whoah shoult teach our Sunday School class for the next three months, they take the better part of a class periot to ficker it aut. And such goin back and forth—(*singsong*) "do ve haff the giffs, does she haff the giffs, does he haff the giffs—vat do youah think, and vat do youah think, and vat do youah think?"

Jake: Mate me plain dissy.

M.J.: That's the vurt—*dissy*. I shoult pay no mind. I shoult have learnt years agoah that these edchakatet vuns can't handle bein wotet doun—so theyah come up with this here vay vere they control the whole thing vith their vurts and systems. I chust vant Elmer twoah teach. But you coult seeah they don't fancy Elmer, do they nowah? But if ve wotet, Elmer voot vin each time.

Jake: You're proply right, Martha Chain.

M.J.: I knowah I'm right.

Jake: So vy didn't ya wolunteer to teach yourself?

M.J.: Me-ah?

Jake: You're a fine teacher.

M.J.: Vell, apart from the fact that there's a bunch of men in the class, it's these here vuns vith their big vurts that allvays floor me.

Jake: Touch of prite, sounts like.

M.J.: I guess maybe. Got me there, Chakie. (*laughs*). But prite's vat ya neet to haff consensus, ain't soah?

Jake: How ya ficker?

M.J.: Vell, if ve all act real humple like, vere's that get us? Huh? Vat I seeah in this consensus baloney is people *asserting* themselves. They act humple, like, "Oh, I don't know if I haff the giffs for this assignment," ant of course Elsie Mae allvays chirps up and says, "But ya doah, ya doah." Then another says, "I'ff been prayin abaut it, but there's no clear answer," and you knowah that Horrelt vill pipe up ant sayah "That's vat community's fer," and then goot olt Elmer says, "It's all right by me if somevun else takes ower," ant dear olt Chorge says, "Vee shoult pray more, vee shoult," and meah, I'm ready to go crazy right there in that room. I come to church to learn, to be blesst, ant if Got vills it, be a blessin to others. But I get so vurkt up insite I think I'm goin to haff a heart attack or go flat aut looney.

Jake: My, myah, it's been a hart morning for youah, Martha Chain.

M.J.: Yes, it has been. But look at youah, Chakie, calm as a cucumber. I hope you're not in no pickle. Consensus don't bother youah none, really?

Jake: I chust go vith the flow.

M.J.: But don't ya vant Elmer to continue?

Jake: That voot be nice.

M.J.: But vat iff Sarah ant her gang take ower the teaching?

Jake: That voot be okayah, too.

M.J.:   That's not consensus.
Jake: Oh, really?
M.J.:   You're chust going along vith things.
Jake: Vat's so wrong abaut that?
M.J.:   Vell, it ain't consensus. I don't like consensus, but vat I'm learnin is that people who like consensus say they vant to submit, but they're offen the assertive type underneath.
Jake: Really?
M.J.:   Yeah, you're not bein assertive, Chakie.
Jake: Vell, somebody has to be nonresistant these days. That's myah part.
M.J.:   (*laughs*) Ya got me there, Chakie, ya got me real goot. See ya next Sunday.
Jake: Now Martha Chain, make me a promise, vonct.
M.J.:   Like vat?
Jake: Promise me ya von't get so steamt up ower little things.
M.J.:   But it ain't little.
Jake: Promise?
M.J.:   Oh, okayah. Now you behaaff, Chakie.
Jake: Youah twoah. See ya later.

Merle Good of Lancaster, Pennsylvania, is a writer, dramatist, publisher, and a co-editor of this volume.

18 Politically Correct Put-Downs

Note to New Mennonites: below is a list of do's and do-not's related to whom and what you may make fun of—if you want to be a respected, politically-correct Mennonite.

OK to Make Fun of
or Put Down

1. plain Mennonites
2. pot pie and borscht
3. conscientious objection to military service
4. secondhand clothing
5. M.B.'s
6. buggies
7. Lancaster bishops
8. opposition to abortion
9. witness to personal faith in Jesus Christ
10. head covering
11. Amish quilts
12. Goshen
13. homemade root beer
14. jeans with holes
15. using the lot for selection of leaders
16. E.M.U.
17. U.S. nationalism
18. bald heads

Definitely Wrong to Make Fun of or Put Down

1. Mennonites with Ph.D's
2. grilled veggies
3. protests to powerful governments
4. brand-name duds
5. G.C.'s
6. S.U.V.'s
7. Transformation leaders
8. opposition to capital punishment
9. vague about Christ
10. rock-climbing gear
11. Ten Thousand Villages
12. Winnipeg
13. Miller-Lite
14. jeans with holes
15. politically-correct voting procedure for pastor selection
16. M.C.C.
17. Canadian nationalism
18. shaved heads

Lyrics in search of a
Mennonite artist to complete —

What shall I do?
  What would be right?
I won the Lottery last night! . . .
          * * *

It was a frisky church retreat
With old Bud Yoder in a heat,
Some prankster dropped Viagra pills
Into Bud's cup of soup for thrills . . .
          * * *

We are inclusive in our hearts
Unless you don't quite fit,
We're all in one, the various parts
Unless you don't quite fit . . .
          * * *

We are for peace,
  We fight for peace,
    Peace may not cease,
      We'll make it so,
        And you should know,
          That even though
            It is not so
              We'll force it so
                Because we know
                  Peace may not cease . . .

Testing Your Consensus Meter

(Circle the correct letter for each statement)

Strongly Agree	Agree	Not Sure	Disagree	Strongly Disagree		
A	B	C	D	E	1.	Mennonites are especially good at forgiveness.
A	B	C	D	E	2.	When a Mennonite tells you that all is forgiven and forgotten, it is the best policy to expect that an unexpected payback is in your future.
A	B	C	D	E	3.	Quakers are better at forgiveness than Mennonites because they have less to forgive.
A	B	C	D	E	4.	Mennonite history proves that forgiveness can be compelled.
A	B	C	D	E	5.	Mennonite children are in general more polite, generous, and agreeable than other children because they have such forgiving parents.

The humorous pieces on pages 180-183 are by Merle Good, Rebecca Good, and Kate Good.

Merle Good, Lancaster, Pennsylvania, is a writer, dramatist, publisher, and a co-editor of this volume. Rebecca Good teaches English in a middle school in Harrisonburg, Virginia. Kate Good is a graduate student in creative writing in Fairfax, Virginia.

Short Fiction, II

End of an Accident

by Carroll D. Yoder

"Would you get my lesson help and Bible on the dining room table?" Mama was pinning on her covering and as usual the last one ready for church. Papa had backed the '47 Ford out of the garage and Russell had already claimed his place by the left back door—the left one because Mama and Little Davy sat in front and Norman would get the right back door. The person on the left side got to church first, home first and was on the driver's side, but for Darrell it wasn't worth a big argument.

"Come on, let's run," Mama said. "Papa doesn't like to be late for church." It wasn't Mama's fault if they were late. She had to dress Davy, finish the dishes, fix her hair and covering and see that the boys had their hair combed decent. Papa did the chores and helped with the dishes. It didn't take long for him to dress— no necktie to bother with.

"It looks like we're going to be late again," Papa said as Mama got in the car.

"Just don't know where the time got to; thought I was up good and early. I walked over to the other house with a bowl of carrot salad for Grandma since she's having us and Lloyd's for dinner and we talked too long."

Darrell liked Sunday dinner at Grandpa's almost as much as getting invited out to somebody else's place where there were children with different toys. Kenny, Twila and Melvin Ray would be at Grandpa's, too.

Mama continued. "And now that a person can't go in during the songs—they keep you waiting on the landing—I hate all the more walking in late, especially when there are four or five verses."

"It's to make people get themselves around on time."

"Turn up that back window," Mama said to Russell. "I can't believe how dry it is."

Dust from a passing car rose to the top of the telephone and high line wires and then settled down over the corn, dulling dark green leaves. The speedometer showed 45; Papa wouldn't drive fast on the dirt road even if the family was late for church.

"O.K. from the east," Norman advised. Gravel scattered as Papa pulled up the sharp incline onto the church road at the T and turned west.

"Watch out!" Mama screamed.

A car, flying up over the little hill beside the graveyard, skidded sideways, scraped a front fender against Papa's left taillight as it swerved on around the side and came to a stop some 25 feet ahead. A moment of silence and then doors opened as the dust cleared.

"Harry Knepp and his folks on the way to church!" Mama said.

"Could've been a lot worse," Papa said.

Russell had hopped out the left door and was looking at the broken pieces of taillight. "Harry's a fast driver," he said.

"Doesn't keep him from being late for church," Mama answered.

The men formed a half circle to discuss the accident.

"I was pushin' it a little," Harry admitted. "Tryin' to get to church on time."

"And I hadn't made it all the way into the right lane when you came sailing over that hill." Papa always gave the other person the benefit of the doubt. "We'll have to talk about it later."

Darrell knew who was to blame for the accident. Papa was just crossing over onto the right side when the Knepp car flew over the graveyard hill, too fast to get stopped. Harry Knepp—driving like a teenager with a father who smoked and maybe even drank. Chester Knepp would slap Grandpa on the back and laugh like he was the best Christian in the world. Grandpa never said a word even if he was the deacon. Just let himself be buttered up.

"Accidents happen," Chester said. "I guess your windows were up because of the dust and you couldn't hear us on the other side of the hill."

"You really got to juice it pulling out of that dirt road," Harry added. His advice made cautious driving sound dangerous. Darrell saw Papa's jaw tighten while he nodded in agreement. The men shook hands and all got back in their cars because they were already late for church. Fortunately the left back fender wasn't rubbing on the wheel, but Darrell knew that he would taste shame when the men lined up their cars along the side of the church house to pick up their families after the service. It was the same feeling he got when he bent his glasses out of shape, missed seeing the egg on his bib overalls until he was in school, or left a stinker by accident next to a girl.

In the car Papa told the family that everything was settled; he would pay the Knepps for the damages on their car. Darrell felt his stomach tighten. "But it wasn't our fault!"

Papa didn't want names in the paper. How would that look with one Mennonite suing another even if it was the insurance companies that were responsible? It would leave a bad witness among the English. Darrell thought it was unfair, but Papa said he didn't know what being a Mennonite had to do with fairness. There was no more discussion. It was the end of the accident.

Carroll D. Yoder, Harrisonburg, Virginia, is an English and French professor, and a writer.

Moments

by Greta Holt

"Not tired, are you?" Marian's voice was muffled, her head emerging from the frost rings of the freezer.

Beth lounged against the door frame. "Nope." She moved her hips an inch as her sister swept past with a cut-glass bowl of white chocolate mousse.

"You don't want to overdo it before a long flight," said Marian.

"Right."

"I mean it. It's 22 hours to New York." Marian shook out the orange and white, hand-printed, birds of Botswana tablecloth.

"I know that."

Marian the Magnificent. Beth watched her sister's deft movements.

"And five hours to Cincinnati with the stop-over." Two spots on a wine glass were annihilated.

Last night, Beth had stuffed her three weeks of treasures into an expandable cloth suitcase. Delicious remembrances of charging hippo and floating giraffe mixed with bulky leatherwork purses and belts from outdoor markets where merchandise marched for blocks on green tarps, and vendors dared customers to eat dried mopani worms. Piles of soft-woven tapestries from the ladies of the Oodi Weavers gently enveloped hordes of ostrich eggs and stashes of lavender agate jewelry.

"Ke bokaee?" (How much?) still pulsed on Beth's eardrums, ruefully accompanied by Tosca's plaintive, *"Quanto?"*

There had been a party at the house each weekend of Beth's visit. Marian had been generous, of course, taking her short vacation from Botswana University so Beth could see the country from an insider's view. Her sister could have been hiking in Drakensberg with a South African Council of Churches deacon and his groupies. People loved being with Marian, The Grand Insider. She always had something going.

"Let's get ready. The concert won't wait, and I have to get back for my guests." Marian stepped to the closet and slung a jasmine and scarlet cape over her shoulders. "It's N'debele; got it in Zimbabwe last year."

"Okay."

On this, Beth's last afternoon in Gaborone, Marian took her over bumpy roads to Mochudi's bright mix of pastel bungalows, thatched rondavels, and sudden bristling hills, to hear the children's rhythm band from the blind school. Beth had grabbed one of their flyers last week as it skittered by her outdoor table-with-shade at the President Hotel on the Mall. The flyer said the blind kids had their own tee-shirts to sell in sky blue with black lettering, Botswana's colors. Staring at the dog-eared brochure, Beth, for no reason she could discern, had decided it essential to hear the blind kids perform. Marian had sighed.

Now, in the second half of the concert, after a stamped and chanted entrance of skillful children and exotic instruments, a volunteer was called for to sing and play along. Marian hauled Beth up and pushed her to the front.

"Stop shoving!"

"Oh, go on. I told them you were good. Go."

Beth kept reasonably in time on what they called a *sivukuvuku* drum (which sounded like a hippopotamus) to a rather overly rhythmic rendition of "Gonna' Lay Down My Burden," and she even found herself improvising a descant and a rhythm, clacking marapo bones together to "We Are Going Through This World on the Way to Heaven." The announcer said the kids were singing it in Setswana, Swahili, and N'debele. For her part, Beth stuck to la,la,la.

"Good job. That descant was a little high, but you handled it."

"Thanks."

Afterward Simon, the little blind drummer pictured passionately pounding bongos on the tee-shirt, touched Beth's hair and murmured, "Veddy soft!" Beth the Enchanted. She decided she wouldn't mind wearing Simon on her chest and spent 30 pula on four shirts. She told herself she'd use the rest for birthday presents.

Marian drove her new Mazda 323 back fast, dodging four scraggly goats, two cows, and a line of matrons balancing bulky, double-decker bundles on their heads. The women's lithe forms, clad in loose blouses and slim skirts seemingly fit for a *Vogue* cover, belied threadbare repairs and practical shoes scuffed by swirling sand. As the car zipped through the city's center, Beth took a last, speedy look at the Mall with its neat, brick courtyard and stone-carved arches.

"Slow down."

"I have guests."

Tonight's party included Marian's professor friends and their spouses. Since Marian taught voice lessons in her free time, her friends decided to perform songs and readings, laughing and clapping for each other. Beth played piano for everyone. The favorite was the economics professor, Gaotse, and her German husband singing "I Love You Truly" and digging each other in the ribs for mistakes.

Ojang, who was soon on his way to Yale, gave a straight-faced rendition of Gilbert and Sullivan's "I Am the Very Model of a Modern Major General," using an upperclass British accent touched with the warm vowels of Setswana. Marian's parody of "Sentimental Journey," complete with a facsimile of a Bakgatla dance in honor of Beth's trip home, was well-received by the company who laughed and sang along.

There was applause for Beth's accompanying skills which she shrugged off. "Oh, I don't play much anymore."

"Yes, you do. You still play piano every other Sunday at Cincinnati Mennonite."

"Thanks, I forgot."

Later, as the party-goers sank into their chairs and further into their wine, the talk turned toward the affairs of Botswana and the world, which translated, as Beth had found, into a discussion of South Africa and apartheid.

"At precisely the very moment the Boer feels the sting of the black scorpion, he will run. Not one moment before. Believe me when I say . . . " John, the white, South African, political refugee, started one of his lengthy speeches. Beth was relieved when Ojang interrupted.

"Moments! That's it. Let's spend Beth's last night with us telling the most important moment in each of our lives. Come on. Everybody is allowed five minutes, no more." Ojang smiled beatifically at his friend, the South African, who replied that his would take seven minutes, thank you ever so much.

Sitting comfortably in the cool of the African winter evening, Beth floated upon the goodwill of Marian's friends. It amazed her that given lousy phone service, only a smattering of radios, and maybe a four-year-old movie at the museum once in a while, her sister's crowd found ways to enjoy each other and to entertain themselves. She knew with bleak certainty that at home she'd be wiped out in front of the TV, telling herself she'd get up in a while and have a life.

Tales of the villages mingled with European cares. Refugee survival stories followed embarrassing moments. Some of their stories were sad, others dramatic, and a few funny.

Hans told of his and Gaotse's first trip across the western savannah to meet her family in remote Ghanzi. They took provisions and liters of water. The so-called roads into the Kalahari were lonely at best. On the way the truck broke down, of course. The tailpipe and most of the bottom came off. Hans and Gaotse were sitting dejectedly on the bonnet of the Mercedes discussing the damage—and deciding how best to protect themselves on an overnight with some of Africa's wildest desert dwellers—when a government vehicle came by and a fine Motswana fellow rescued them as quickly as one could hope. As the three were bumping toward Ghanzi, Hans asked the young man how often he passed that way. "Quite often," he answered happily. "Every four months."

Ojang told of his life-defining encounter with an
amorous, or angry, Cape buffalo. In the dusk of the
delta it was hard to tell which, he said. "My opinion
of humanity's legs improved that day forever. The
agility of my limbs is a thing of wonder." Ojang flexed
his skinny muscles, soliciting snickers from his audi-
ence.

Beth plumped an Indian elbow pillow on the
Swedish-made couch. What a group. Typical
Botswana: every kind of accent, a shared purpose in
keeping a new country going. It was so fresh, so good.
She wondered for the thousandth time what awaited
her back home.

"Okay, mine?" Beth said. "All right. I would have to
say my major moment was back in '66."

"Uh-oh. Settle in. I know this one: the Anabaptist
moment—no, the whole movement—in a nutshell. It
takes a while." Marian smiled.

"So, let me tell it then."

Beth spun her story. She had used it often to illus-
trate the '60s to her junior high history classes. She
wondered if it made her sound like a knee-jerk liberal. But she kept telling it; the kids said they liked it,
or they liked the class time it took up.

"I remember faces exploding into shouts, and the
sky dark with rocks and bottles. And noise like a tidal
wave. We whites, just a group of young volunteers,
didn't belong there. Some of the black marchers did-
n't even want us along. When anybody on our side
fell, they were stuffed into vans, and the vans could-
n't get through."

"Where was this?" Gaotse asked.

"Chicago." Marian put down her drink and yawned.

Beth shrugged. "We turned a corner. All of a sudden, we were right beside 'the whites.' I didn't feel like one of them that day."

She warmed to her subject. "I saw it coming from a couple feet away, but I couldn't stop moving forward. We were taught to fall and roll in a ball if we got attacked. There was a group of men, drunk. One man brought up spit from his throat and let it go. It hit my left temple and ran down the side of my face.

"Suddenly someone touched my wrist. A young man, a black from one of the gangs. Chicago gang members were getting the worst of it that day. They'd been taking the rocks and bottles on themselves, trying to protect the marchers. They hadn't fought back; they'd just been there. The white men backed away."

"See! It's the black worker who will have to do it all." John, the South African, was enthralled.

"S-s-sh!"

"Quiet."

"All day we marched through that mess. Finally, as we neared the dividing line of the white and black neighborhoods, I saw a few black men on their porches with hunting guns. You hardly ever saw blacks with guns back then. The white crowd disappeared. Gone!" Beth raised an eyebrow meaningfully at the group. "We'd done our job all day with nonviolence, with prayer, and the whites ran away at the sight of blacks with guns."

"Two minutes," said Marian looking at her watch.

"Okay, okay. We wandered around in the neighborhood Baptist churchyard, drinking in the silence, trying not to duck when birds flew over or a piece of paper fluttered by."

"I thought it was an Ana-Baptist moment," some-body said.

"Anti-Baptist?"

"Hush!"

Beth pushed on. "I found myself standing on a stairway with a black woman. She and I looked at each other, just looked.

"I felt—I don't know—a great weight lift from me. In that moment, that really special moment, time stopped. My shoulders felt light, almost as if I were floating. The woman and I sank onto the stoop; we smiled.

"Then my friends called me and I left. The moment came and went, but it felt good, right.

"So, that's my most important moment." Beth tipped her head back and polished off her drink. "That or the time my half-slip fell off while I was dancing the part of the Rainbow Fairy in sixth grade; they still talk about it at reunions."

The laughter was gratifying, but Beth had the feeling, as always, she hadn't communicated.

It wasn't about race, at least she didn't think so. It was the simplicity of the moment that fascinated her.

"Okay, but I am just asking what is the Anabaptist part?" Gaotse looked around daring anyone to shush her.

"Martyrdom." Marian stretched. "Smash yourself against the evil beings, and gain epiphany."

"*I* didn't say it was Anabaptist," Beth mumbled.

She had come close to feeling that good about life only a few other times: scrubbing a pot until its reflection sparkled in a stream near a campfire; playing the last perfect chord of a fast, contrapuntal Bach variation on an organ at full volume; reaching the summit of Mount Washington in horizontal sleet with a 40-pound pack on her back. Time had not mattered. Deed attempted, deed accomplished. Clear, simple, clean.

For her turn at moments, Marian talked about nearly crawling with fear into her doctoral orals. Everybody clapped because, as Marian told her story, most of this group hoped for their doctorates, too.

"Great, wonderful, good for all," Beth said.

After a few toasts, the party broke up. Beth had an early travel day tomorrow, Marian insisted. Everyone said Beth should visit again. They complimented her piano-playing and wished her well on her trip home. She was told how wonderful it was to work with her sister.

Ojang said John and he would go out on the town for some late-night revelry. John muttered something about writing to Beth, and he actually kissed her hand. John the Intense. He looked so serious, Ojang laughed and dragged him out.

"So my life's a cliché. I never said it wasn't." Beth shifted to a more comfortable position on the couch after the guests left. "But I stayed and worked with kids, not like you. You ran off to hang around the elite, the intellectuals. Look at all this. Your life's a breeze. You wouldn't know a discipline problem if it hit you."

"I hear you, Miss Dramatic. You've been griping at me for days. Get to the point." Marian gathered plates and glasses from around the room. "No? Number one, you planned your own life, and number two, after a while you got sick of working with poor kids and went to work in a rich school like everybody else."

"Yeah, the good school, where the kids aren't aggressive to your face. Their daddies' lawyers just send you little notes."

"Do you ever stop complaining?"

"No." Beth rubbed the pressure point in her forehead with the palm of her hand. "But my life's been filled with stuff. Just stuff."

"So what, Beth? Everybody's life is a mess. Ojang wants to believe in grand moments? Fine. Pointless, but fine." Marian swept Beth's glass from the side table. She tossed a wet dishtowel at her sister. "Get your psycho-babble fanny up and help."

Beth rose and leaned on the counter. "You think you've figured everything out." She rubbed at a spoon until it squeaked. "Everything here is so, well, so meaningful."

"Whatever that means."

Beth flipped the towel at Marian's arm, and launched the forgotten spoon over Marian's right shoulder. It clattered in the sink. "Oops." A little unsteady, she poured herself the remainder of the wine.

Funny how Marian and she hadn't mentioned the drinking; it seemed that everybody in the whole world drank, now. Or maybe in the past years, Beth herself had simply begun to see the world through the ironic lens of a city girl. Beth was embarrassed to discover that the small college town of idealists where Marian and she had grown up seemed quainter each year. Certainly, Marian was corrupted; her bread was buttered by Botswana University, not the religious community here: not by her own people.

"Little sister, your life is your choice." Marian patted Beth's head.

"Don't patronize me."

"Don't act like you need it."

Beth swirled the purple wine around the bottom of her glass. The wine made a slick, ever-changing film on the glossy surface. She spoke slowly. "Say, Marian, what if I were to come here to live? They need teachers, lots of them. The number of schools is growing, and I'm very, very good." The color of wine sloshing at the bottom of her glass drifted from slippery plum to indigo. "I should get in on this before they decide they don't want us anymore. You know, *us* outsiders."

When she looked up, Marian was staring at her open-mouthed. The two frown lines on her forehead were so deep, African termites could hide in them.

"Okay. Geeze." Beth grinned.

Marian didn't.

"All right, take a pill." Beth sailed from the room, leaving Marian to clean up; she sipped her wine in a long, hot shower. There was a drought on, but she didn't care, not one bit.

Marian was waiting when she came out. "Towel off your hair. We're going out dancing."

"This late?"

"Well, I'm not going to stay here and listen to you crab, especially since this is your *last* night in Botswana." Marian gave her a flat look.

"I'm not crabbing, I'm thinking outloud."

Nothing Beth said would discourage Marian from dancing at the disco on the outskirts of the capital. The car sped past jumbles of roadside trash. Carelessly thrown cups and cigarettes fronted spotless, whitewashed cottages. They arrived before midnight in a flotilla of slightly worn Peugots and

Citroens. Something by the BeeGee's pounded
through the dancers on the bare wood floor. Couples
and linedancers gyrated among the twirling colored
lights. Beth and Marian were grabbed firmly around
the waist and propelled toward the center of the
room.

Ojang led the sisters in hip-breaking fashion to
"Stayin' Alive." Beth laughed; it was June 13, 1985,
and Africa was just catching disco fever.

"John and I couldn't go home! Too much nightlife
in the metropolis," he shouted.

"You're just excited about Yale," Marian yelled
back.

"No-o-o kidding!" he crooned.

Beth watched him sweep into the spinning crowd
of pounding pelvises. Ojang the Elegant.

The sisters found a table and ordered Appletizers.
They kept to safe topics and safer drinks.

"Did you see the drums the blind boy played this
afternoon?" The little drummer from the band had
floated into Beth's mind more than once this evening.
"Veddy soft," he'd whispered.

"Simon? His picture's on their tee-shirt."

"I know that. But, did you notice his drums were
old, cracked? I sure can't tell all the kinds of drums
they had, but I know that much. And they had holes in
the drumheads. Doesn't anybody pay their expenses?"

"It's all donations." Marian fished out a lighter. "Do
you know some are blind because of measles? Didn't
catch it in time."

"That's awful."

"Beth," Marian watched a colorful couple tango by
as she tapped out a cigarette. The woman's skirts

tossed out a dark, spicy perfume, and the man pulled her fast to his hip as they turned. "Why don't you stop romanticizing and just live? You know, as in minute by minute."

Beth plucked Marian's unlit cigarette, sniffed it, and wrinkled her nose. "As in getting the job done, and paying the bills, and dealing with difficult people?" She eyed her sister. "Not evil, just boringly difficult people?"

"Yes, and I deal with them here." Marian swiped at the cigarette. "You keep forgetting I've been on vacation all this time, with you."

"Yeah, I know my head's in the clouds."

"So get your feet on the ground."

Beth tossed the cigarette across the table. She rested her chin on her hand and stuck out her lower lip. "My type is a mistake, an error, an anomaly."

"Oh, brother."

Beth executed an expansive shrug. She watched Marian stroke the lighter to life. The smoke from Marian's cigarette glided toward the high thatched ceiling and was carried away by a Latin beat.

"Why, in heaven's name, did you ever start that?" Beth said. "It's so dumb it's a sin."

"At least I don't eat like there's no tomorrow."

"Lung-buster."

"Butterball."

Ojang low-dipped a pretty Motswana girl in front of their table and ended with a dashing flamenco flourish. He dismissed her with a wave of his hand and sat with the sisters.

"Dear ladies, I am begging for a lift home. I see John, my South African friend and my lift, leaving with a very good-looking woman. Too old for him, but he doesn't care. He wants to forget everything. Look at that, he doesn't wave. He's so nervous lately, he's giving me craziness."

"Why?" Beth felt a little hurt. John the Unfaithful.

Ojang shrugged. "He thinks South African commandos are looking for him and the other refugees. He examines every package he gets for bombs."

"John has a martyr complex and a big head," Marian explained. "He thinks he's on every blacklist the South African police have, but he's not even ANC."

"No, but he does have appropriately shady connections with the trade unions."

"The South African army wouldn't come up here, would it?" asked Beth.

Ojang leaned forward in an exaggerated whisper. "We're awfully close to the border, and we're probably sitting beside tables of spies right now."

Beth tried not to stare at the groups nearby. People of all races mixed and mingled. Blue-eyed blondes bumped hips with black-eyed browns; colors flashed and twined. Laughter and caresses blended in strong, steady coffee-and-cream rhythms.

To Beth's right, though, was an all-white group. Beefy men, they were drinking silently, purposefully. Boer Bullies? Afrikaner Assault Troops?

"Hey, stop scaring me," she whispered to Ojang. "I have to fly down to Johannesburg and go through their rip-through-your-baggage customs tomorrow."

Ojang looked properly horrified. He glanced around dramatically.

"I won't visit you at your great, snotty Yale if you don't stop it," Beth said.

"I'm sorry. I'm so excited." Ojang looked happy. "But, ladies, you must share with me your considerable knowledge of U.S. life so I may be a famous success."

It was well past midnight, June 14, when they left. They drove in friendly silence up the road toward town. My last night in Botswana, Beth thought. The African moon is beautiful, so much clearer than at home.

Even the trash on the roadside glowed sapphire in the pristine light. Crumpled flyers and paper bags tumbled with sudden gusts of wind.

"No one is passing!" A loud-hailer shattered the air. "No one is passing!"

The searchlight blinded them.

Marian froze at the wheel, her foot on the gas.

Gunfire pounded nearby, and another car ran into the back of them.

"Marian, stop!" Beth screamed.

Bullets ripped at the top of the car. The windshield cracked.

"Get the bloody hell out of that car!"

An explosion ruptured their world.

"Who are they?" Beth's voice keened to a howl.

Ojang lunged from the back seat and pulled the key from the ignition. "We've got to get out, now," he whispered. "Let's go!" He yanked the door handle and pushed Marian. "Get out."

"Wait!" Beth stumbled out of the passenger side. She waved wildly. "American! I'm American!"

On the other side of the car, a boy behind Marian spun and fell. Bullets sprayed flying sand like shrapnel. Marian screamed and threw her hands over her eyes.

"No one is passing!"

Beth clawed and kicked her body awkwardly over the hood of the car. She bore Marian's weight as they staggered from the road. Rough laughter and gunfire followed them. She made out "kafir" in the shouting.

Ojang pointed to a low protection wall and they veered toward it. A man running nearby spit air and gasped as another round hit. All of them fell over the wall.

"Bloody Boers." The man held his side and crawled away.

"Marian?" Beth pulled Marian's hands away from her face.

"I—I think it's sand; it's in my eyes. I can't see." Marian's voice shook.

Beth swiped at the left side of her sister's face. "Keep crying. It might wash some of the sand out." She brushed Marian's hair back with unsteady fingers.

"I'm not crying. Ow, dammit."

They moved along the wall of the house, then, watching the road, bolted from house to house.

"We've got to get her to hospital!" Ojang hissed. "Give her to me." With Marian between them, they made better time. They could hear explosions from far off, even as armored trucks roared down on them.

"Tlokweng Road. They're on their way home, and we never even heard them come," Ojang whispered.

"What are they doing here?"

"South Africans." Ojang swore. "Looking for ANC. Maybe for protesters. They'll kidnap them, kill them. They're not going to care who else they hurt."

"I need to rest." Marian stumbled. "Just a little."

Beth saw large acacias ahead in front of a bullet-pocked dwelling. The house was in flames. The top of one of the acacias smoldered, then flared and showered them with sparks. They scrambled to the safer tree and collapsed.

Beth started to shake. She saw they were all slick with sweat in the cold night air. She ripped off her sweater and tried to wipe Marian's face carefully. The sand might as well have been shards of glass. "Can you see anything?"

"Stop it. Maybe a little out of my left eye, but I don't want to keep it open." Marian sighed as Ojang wrapped his coat around her. Beth cradled Marian's head in her lap. They huddled together in the light of the fire from the burning house and listened to the roaring engines and staccato of the retreating troops. Distant explosions throbbed through the ground and crept along their backbones.

"Beth?" Ojang said finally, catching his breath.

"Yes."

Ojang placed his hand on her shoulder. "Beth. I just must ask you this and please do not be angry. Please. I just wish to know, what is this, 'I'm an American!'?"

"What?"

"An American. Is it like when John Wayne says to drop your drawers and hand over your weapons?" Ojang made a sound like a laugh or a sob. He squeezed her shoulder. "I'm sorry."

Beth stared at him. She balled her fists and gulped air. How could he be making fun of her? Jesus Christ Almighty, his country was being invaded. Jerk. Creep.

"Beth?"

"Yes, Marian. I'm here, honey. What do you need?"
Beth leaned down to hear her sister better.

Marian said weakly, "Why didn't you sing 'God
Bless America,' and save us all?"

Beth snorted. All three dissolved in laughter.
Holding tightly to each other, they gasped and cried.
Tears from the smoke and tension stained their faces
into bizarre masks. A truck roared by and they could
hear shouting and sporadic gunshots. They ducked.

"Run back across the border, cowards," Ojang
hissed.

It was suddenly silent. Only the steady crackle of
the fire could be heard. Beth and Ojang leaned their
backs against the smooth grain of the tree trunk. They
inhaled the cool, calm Kalahari night air, borne by a
west wind. Beth ran her hands gently through
Marian's hair. Their breathing turned toward normal,
and Ojang tried humming a sketchy tune. Tiredly,
Beth imagined it sounded like something from Gilbert
and Sullivan: " . . . and everyone will say, as I walk
my mystic way . . . " By squinting, she could see a
few stars far beyond the firesparks.

"Auntie, Uncle, help me! I'm in here!" The cry rode
the flames of the house next door. A child's voice.
"Please, help me!"

Beth and Ojang looked at one another a moment.
Ojang's face was rigid, "I—"

"Don't go," Marian whispered. "Shells lying
around." She clutched at Beth's skirt. "Don't. Beth,
don't!"

But Beth felt a smile play at the corners of her eyes.
She was leading the blind children's band at full contrapuntal volume up a stormswept mountain, in hori-

zontal rain, to the beat of a sparkly new red drum.
Beth the Bold. Simon the Unsighted.

Clear, clean.

Beth rose. She laid her sweater carefully over
Marian's face. "Take care of my sister."

Ojang cradled Marian to protect her from the sand
that flew back as Beth's feet cut deep patterns into
the earth.

Greta Holt is a writer living in Cincinnati, Ohio.

Poetry, II

Rain

by Jeff Gundy

And a stray face spins me back to the black-haired
    girl
I saw long ago and stood helpless
watching her pass, bareheaded in the rain,
the easy way she found, wet but not hunched
against it, hair damp and shining on her brow,
her shoulders. I wanted to give something
for the dark rain of that hair,
the quiet of her face, not angry or restless,
alert to each step, the crowded sidewalk . . .
But what? Words? Dark rain. Wet face.

She never saw me. We've tramped on down
our own dark tunnels now for years. What hapless
    watcher
at my gates would know her face, would let her in
without the password, find her a bed, say rest,
sleep, I'll be outside?

I know. It shouldn't matter
who's lovely in the rain and who isn't.
But it's not beauty or nostalgia or even lust
that's got me, I don't know what it is,
justice maybe, prisons and churches, the glowing
    creatures

in the center of the sun. Most days I think
I'm almost free, I don't miss a single meeting,
I don't hit squirrels with my bike. Most days
it doesn't rain, and nobody walks the streets
in black hair, a light jacket and a glaze
of shining water, rain beading and touching her
all over like the hand of someone very large
and very gentle, very far away.

Jeff Gundy is a poet and professor living and writing in Bluffton, Ohio.

Claiming the Dust

by Jean Janzen

Like nomads we come
to this subtropical valley,
our borrowed space
under the sun. Once
an ancient lakebed,
the July ground powders
under our feet, lifts
in puffs to welcome us.
The children rise, then
run out to pound acorns
under the oaks, calling
to each other from
their rings of stones.
Pale bird-of-paradise leans
out of its gravelly bed.
It takes dynamite to plant
an orange tree, our neighbor sighs.

This is our new home,
this valley's layered clay
which offers its sunbaked surface
to the scuffing of our feet,
as if our fragile lives
are enough to rouse the ages.
The slightest breeze, and the dust
becomes skittish, whirls

to settle in the next yard.
But mostly, stillness,
so that the beige siftings
are almost imperceptible.
Fig leaves in a talcum haze.

It is the night we finally learn
to claim. At dusk the children
float their sheets like flattened tents
and sprawl face-up into the warm
darkness, and we join them
in this rehearsal—a summer
night travel, the sky's black
curtains pinned back with stars.
That open stage.
This hard earth not our final holding
place after all, but the air
into which we sail,
breath by dusty breath,
toward a different shore.

Jean Janzen is a poet living and writing in Fresno,
California.

today

by Sarah Klassen

i will live quite simply
as if the hand's clenched fingers
could be persuaded to let go
open like petals of a rose

as if this treacherous lake could bear me
on its rough skin
water come tumbling from a rock
demons from a troubled woman

as if there's a fair chance
coin-stacked tables could be over turned
the caged bedraggled dove released
the lethal wind beguiled by evening
and by god the dead raised

Sarah Klassen, Winnipeg, Manitoba, is a poet, writer, and editor.

Sestina for Liars and Thieves

by Rhoda Janzen

The sky began to blush the shade of modest red
of an offended heroine with honor stolen.
How could I avoid shelling peas? I could lie
about certain urgencies, and linger in the outhouse
until sunset dropped fragile on the corn
like the invitation of a lady's handkerchief.

Beggarman, thief, doctor, lawyer, Indian Chief—
A hysterical little moon would finish the red
that the sky was crying over the fields of corn.
The light was dying: so little time to be stolen!
(I kept a cache of stories behind the outhouse.)
It wasn't that I wanted to deceive—I *had* to lie

about the outhouse, where pleasure could belie
all else. And anyway, I spread a rosebud kerchief,
lavender-scented (purloined from the Liebelts' house),
across my nose, or held my breath until I turned red
as well-water with mineral secrets stolen
from the earth, sweet under fields of corn.

WHAT MENNONITES ARE THINKING, 2001

Opening a book was like husking corn:
the leaves turned back over gold that could lie
snug as wishes, or like big pale doubloons stolen
by brigands about to double-cross their chief.
Harvest plumped the wheat, turned it red . . .
and still I lingered in the house

of fiction that I built outside the outhouse.
My books husked worlds like ears of corn
stripped right down to a private part, all red.
I saw how it would end. I would learn to lie
and wave deception like a lacy handkerchief—
Yoo-hoo!—when something's lost or stolen,

but innocently, as if I didn't know what I had stolen.
When light failed, I would slip back to the house,
where I folded fantasy into a plain cotton kerchief;
and like a good girl ate my greens and corn,
nearly fifty years ago. Why should the mirror lie?
Now sometimes when I write, the ink leaks a red

warning—twilight, twilight! Words read and stolen
lie like a tiny house in which a wife, by lamplight,
husks the corn's silk kerchief, sweet as any heroine.

Rhoda Janzen, Holland, Michigan, is a poet and professor
teaching creative writing.

Leadership #20

by Rich Foss

A leader knows how to be close to loam,
a loose mixture of loss, death, and microbes.

A leader makes room for a falling tree.

Now don't get me wrong;
I love energy, creativity, and joy,
and I long like a pruned raspberry bush longs
but a leader knows how to sit alone
when the tree falls.

He knows that in the decay
a few words will wriggle free
and he will be able to say who he is.

*Rich Foss is a pastor, novelist, and poet in Tiskilwa,
Illinois.*

Leadership #24

by Rich Foss

Short words will not do
and neither will elastic polysyllables.

A leader needs the summer of the long touch.

Be still, lie on your back,
wrapped in the smell of timothy, sweet clover and
blue grass.

It takes long roots to grow something
worth talking about.

*Rich Foss is a pastor, novelist, and poet in Tiskilwa,
Illinois.*

My People

by Cheryl Denise

My people are quiet
and don't always say
what they want
what they need
they leave things off
for you to figure out.

They read bibles and think a lot
but would never tell you their thoughts
unless asked
and even then
they would speak quietly
with a slow strong sense
of who God is.
They'll ask what you believe
and listen.

My people say they don't make oatmeal rolls
as good as Grandma,
even Grandma says this.
My people make carrot juice
and like it.
My Grandpa, who's blind
can play pool
and beat you.

WHAT MENNONITES ARE THINKING, 2001

We eat at long fancy tables
with cloth napkins
and say grace before meals.
Mom makes pumpkin soup
with a little—a little more
maple syrup.

My people eat rich candy
creamy chocolates
not cheap Hershey Kisses
we're talking real love
raspberry truffles
Lindor hazelnut creams.

My people love to feed church visitors
their children's friends
Mrs. Brubacher in the nursing home
even their homosexual neighbor.
Everyone needs food.
Good food
from Sittlers' Bakery in Conestoga
the Old Order women in the kitchen
rolling sweet dough
bosoms cloudy with flour.

My people think the only sin
God really doesn't care about
is gluttony with good food.

My people drink
fresh squeezed orange juice
in the morning
use half-and-half
always have four different kinds of bread
in their kitchens.

They talk of things they don't agree with
or understand
liberals, Catholics, ultraconservatives,
the Daves, blacks
but when they meet one
they offer shoofly pie
and a coffee
a little conversation
and afterwards they'll say
well that one was okay.

My people don't understand your people
but we'll feed you.

Cheryl Denise is a poet living in Philippi, West Virginia.

A Longer Essay

Community—
Creating the Bond

by Dale Schrag

*Dale Schrag gave this presentation to the Mennonite
Educators Conference in September, 2001.*

A homily on paradox

A friend of mine once suggested that a faith that
cannot deal with paradox is a faith not worth having.
He said it over 15 years ago, and I can still remember
where he and I were sitting when he said it. I find
myself coming back to his statement over and over
again.

And why not? After all, everywhere we look in life
we confront paradoxes, contradictions, tensions. There
is the tension between brutal honesty and maintaining
a relationship. There is the tension between protecting one's children and allowing them to gain their
independence. For teachers, there is sometimes the
tension between being liked by your students and
truly teaching. For administrators, there is the
omnipresent tension between trying to protect each
individual employee while at the same time looking
out for the good of the institution.

These tensions, of course, do not disappear when
we move into the realm of religion. If anything, they
intensify. There is the tension between Martin

Luther's recognition of the centrality of grace and the Anabaptists' affirmation of the call to discipleship. There is tension between the Roman Catholic celebration of God in window and song and statue and Ulrich Zwingli's rejection of idols and icons. There is tension between the Southern Baptists' enthusiasm in worship and the Quakers' quiet waiting for the Spirit. And who knows, there may even be tension between singing hymns and singing praise songs.

There is the tension between the God of judgment and the God of love. There is the tension between the call to be a prophet and the need to be a reconciler; between the need to comfort the afflicted and the call to afflict the comfortable. There is the tension between the need to acknowledge our brokenness and the need to celebrate our personhood. And there is always the tension between rejecting the sin and accepting the sinner.

So how should we respond? Our initial, human impulse is to resolve the tension by determining that one way is right and the other is wrong. That will not work. I believe, instead, that we must live *in* the tension—perhaps even celebrate it, keeping it as tight as possible as we do our brief balancing act on the high-wire of life. For the one pole always works as a corrective to the other.

So embrace the tension. For it may help you maintain your balance as you try to inch your way along that narrow footpath of Christ.

There are three paradoxes that I think have critical implications for community, both community in our world and community in our schools. The first I call the paradox of the community tent, the second is the

paradox of humility, the third is the paradox of
Christian discipleship.

The paradox of the community tent

I'm quite confident that the very concept of community encompasses a myriad of paradoxes, but I
want to focus on one, a critical one, a biblical one. It
is found in Isaiah chapter 54, verse 2: "Enlarge the
site of your tent, and let the curtains of your habitations be stretched out; do not hold back; lengthen
your cords and strengthen your stakes."

I am fully aware of the fact that I am taking this
verse out of context. Verses 1 and 3 make quite clear
that Isaiah is talking here about increasing the size of
the family, about having a bunch of babies, not about
building community in the sense that I am using the
term. But I want to apply the metaphor to how we go
about building community in our schools.

The verse holds an apparent paradox. For we are
asked, on the one hand, to "stretch the curtains of our
habitations," to let *more* people in, to let more *different*
and *diverse* people in. And we are simultaneously asked
to "strengthen the stakes," to clarify and commit anew
to that which is foundational. I think our human tendency is to do one or the other, but not both.

On stretching the curtains

Some of us educators, I suspect, are more comfortable stretching the curtains of our habitation than we
are strengthening the stakes. I think the culture of
academia leads us in that direction. Tolerance and
openness to new ideas are key concepts in the culture
of academe. Certain philosophical currents lead us in

that direction. With its proscription against meta-narratives and any absolute truths, postmodernism would seem to be all about stretching the curtains of our habitation. And, let's admit it, economic necessity provides a strong incentive for all of us to stretch the curtains of our habitation.

And we are *called* to stretch the curtains of our habitation. That's a good thing. The church calls it evangelism. Meaningful community demands diversity. Mennonite schools—like the Mennonite church—must be intentionally, proactively, open.

I am not trying to be critical of the Mennonite Board of Education policy on recommended percentages of Mennonite students and faculty in Mennonite schools. We have sufficient theological, racial, ethnic, and cultural diversity within the broader Mennonite church to keep our Mennonite percentages intact—or even raise them—and still be much, much more diverse institutions than we are.

I embrace the call for intentional openness not on pragmatic grounds (that is, since there aren't enough Mennonites to go around, we'd better be open), but on educational and theological grounds.

Parker Palmer in *The Courage to Teach* discusses the "grace of great things." These "great things" are "the subjects around which the circle of seekers has always gathered—not the disciplines that study these subjects, not the texts that talk about them, not the theories that explain them, but the things themselves" [107]. And "we invite diversity into our community," says Palmer, "not because it is politically correct but because diverse viewpoints are demanded by the manifold mysteries of great things" [107].

Conversely, says Palmer, it is the "fear of the live encounter," the "fear of diversity," that allow us to "maintain the illusion that we possess the truth about ourselves and our world" [37]. So we avoid diversity. And Palmer contends that the resulting homogeneity feeds an arrogance [37], an absolutism, a triumphalism that "claims to know precisely the nature of great things, so there is no need to continue in dialogue with [the great things]—or with each other" [109].

Quite a number of years ago when I was still a librarian, I developed rather close relationships with two students—two bright, thoughtful, quite liberal students, neither of whom was Mennonite, both of whom found themselves powerfully attracted to the Mennonite faith. One eventually chose to be baptized and to this day is a passionate Mennonite, active in his local congregation and conference. The other chose to stick with her Presbyterian roots and is today a Presbyterian pastor. In our extended conversations, we frequently focused on what each perceived to be the absence of grace in Mennonite theology. Some time after graduation, I received the following in a letter from the Presbyterian:

"Dale, the issue that concerns me is the Anabaptist view of sin. For me, the realization of my constant propensity to sin is what necessitates my salvation. I will always tend to sin (the human condition, I think), and it is this nature that puts the source of my rescue necessarily outside myself. With such an emphasis on adherent behavior and right action, it seems that those early Anabaptists could not have been taking the sinful nature of human beings seriously. I don't understand how you can take grace seriously unless you know how much you need it by taking sin seriously, and how can you be taking sin seriously if you're thinking you can eventually 'act perfectly'?"

I submit that without that kind of conversation about great things, our schools will be markedly poorer places.

I am convinced as well that, at the congregational level, there is much more theological and sociological sameness in the Mennonite church today than there was in the sixteenth century. Perhaps there is even more than in the latter half of the twentieth century.

I think a growing number of Mennonites assume that the church's primary task is to fulfill their individual spiritual needs. Their primary commitment isn't to the congregation; it is to themselves. So if the congregation hires a pastor that is "theologically incorrect" (or even less than ideal) from their point of view, they'll quickly begin shopping for a new congregation. They will find a church more to their liking. The net result, of course, is that over time you have churches composed primarily of like-minded people.

If and when they meet to do the hard work of discerning what discipleship means, or how to interpret a troubling scripture passage, funny thing—they all have the same idea! I question whether that constitutes a discerning community. It may be little more than individualism writ large. You recall that Parker Palmer suggested that such ideological homogeneity could easily contribute to arrogance and triumphalism. One has to wonder if this growing homogeneity of congregations in the Mennonite church has not contributed to the increasingly rancorous tone of letters in the Mennonite press.

I do not think diversity is a problem. Diversity matters in both church and school. I happen to believe it is something to be treasured. Something to be committed to. I believe our schools ought to be intentionally, proactively open. That's not the problem. The problem is that when we commit to being intentionally open, our tendency is not to strengthen our stakes, but to loosen or weaken them. We have a hard time embracing this paradox in Isaiah 54:2. Why?

We are trying, of course, to be sensitive. We don't want to offend those whose beliefs may be different than ours. No one would deny that "sensitivity is a good thing," but "making ourselves silent is not" [Bryant Myers, *Walking With the Poor,* 225]. Some would argue that silence about things that matter can rightly be interpreted as a kind of insult. Miroslav Volf notes that "religions make truth claims about what constitutes the good life. So if a Muslim is trying to persuade you to embrace Islam, he is not so much meddling in your private affairs as honoring you as a person to whom truth matters. If he had no desire for you to become a Muslim, you could rightly protest that he was either indifferent to your well-being or [indifferent] to his own faith" ["Unaggressive evangelism," *Christian Century,* August 15-22, 2001, p.26].

It's an interesting thought, but I suspect that those of us on the "intentionally open" side of the paradox remain unconvinced.

On strengthening stakes

I once heard a very wise man say that as he grew older, he found himself feeling less and less certain about more and more things; issues that he once thought were open and shut cases now seemed much more complicated and much more complex. But, this wise man added, he was also now much more certain about a few things than he had ever been in his life.

Here, I think, is a principle. As we seek to discern what is foundational for our institutions, what constitutes the "stakes" that secure the tent, we should look for those few things about which we are very certain. Each institution needs to determine (in community) what its "stakes" are. Let me suggest two things about which I am very certain: First, that Mennonite schools need to be explicitly Christian. Second, that Mennonite schools need to be unapologetically Mennonite.

These should both be self-evident truths, but I think they both deserve some explication. Remember that the educational establishment in this country has no time for either one of these positions. George Marsden has noted that while 90% of Americans claim to believe in God, that almost 67% affirm the essentials of Christian orthodoxy, and that at least 33% would qualify as "serious" Christians, virtually all Americans assume that education should happen in a context of "nonbelief"—that our students should learn and our teachers should teach in a manner that in no way explicitly acknowledges the existence of God [Marsden's presentation to the Denominational Executives in Church Related Higher Education, Washington, D.C., 21 April 1999].

So why should we teach in a manner that explicitly acknowledges the existence of God? I am convinced that if we want to create meaningful and lasting community in our schools, we simply must embrace and

acknowledge a transcendent God. Instead of a complicated and logical argument here, I will simply try to
make my case with a personal story.

On 26 May 1991, I was sitting in the Trinitatiskirche
in Wolfenbuttel, Germany. I had come to Wolfenbuttel
three weeks earlier to participate in a research project
at the Herzog August Bibliothek, one of Europe's truly
spectacular libraries. But I had learned immediately
that my German was barely 25% as good as I had
thought it was, I had discovered that I was very poorly
prepared to do the research that I was being asked to
do, and I was alone. My family was to join me in a couple of weeks, but for the past 20-some days (a period
that had seemed like 20-some weeks), I had been
alone—more alone than at any time in my life. I was
isolated by a language I only partially comprehended,
intimidated by a task that seemed beyond my capabili-
ties in almost every respect, clinging desperately to the
hope that I would see my family again.

When I entered the church on that Sunday morning, I knew immediately that something was different.
On my first three visits to Lutheran churches in
Wolfenbuttel, I had been most impressed by their
emptiness. Structures built to accommodate upwards
of 5- to 700 worshippers generally held about 50. This
day, however, was different. By the time the service
began there were over 200 persons present. It was
Familiensonntag (Family Sunday), and the children
were putting on a little dramatic skit based on the
story of Jonah.

It was encouraging to see a German church semi-
full for a change. I clearly perceived the presence of
familial love, some sense of community. But some-

thing was missing for me. I ached for evidence of transcendence. I pined for epiphany, for a "manifestation of God." I wanted desperately to hear at least a liturgical expression with which I could identify. I wanted to hear the *Kyrie Eleison* or the Apostle's Creed or the Lord's Prayer, standard features of every German Lutheran service, but apparently displaced on this day to make room for the children's performance.

I wanted something to transcend the particularity of that *Gemeinschaft*, that community, because, however meaningful and beautiful it was to those assembled, it somehow was a *Gemeinschaft* that did not include me; a *Gemeinschaft*, in fact, that only served to intensify my feelings of loneliness and alienation.

Then finally, at the very end of the service, it came. The Lord's Prayer. The *Vaterunser*. Awash with feelings of gratitude, I joined in. *Vater unser im Himmel. Geheiligt werde dein Name. Dein Reich komme. Dein wille geschehe wie im Himmel, so auf Erden . . .* But my voice broke at that point, and the tears came forth, as I was overcome by a sense of transcendence, overcome by at least a foretaste of epiphany, overcome by the fact that for the first time during that entire service, I too had become a member of the *Gemeinschaft*.

In her book *Amazing Grace*, Kathleen Norris notes that church congregations and monasteries are the two most ancient forms of Christian community. At least in the case of monasteries, she suggests that there is a striking level of diversity among the monks. "Anyone who knows a monastery well," says Norris, "knows that it is no exaggeration to say that you find Al Franken and Rush Limbaugh living next door to each other. Barney Frank and Jesse Helms" (158). So how do they stay living and working and eating and playing together for 50 years? "They know," Norris writes, "that their primary ministry is prayer, and that prayer transcends theological differences" [Ibid.].

In his rule, St. Benedict insisted that monks say the Lord's Prayer together a minimum of three times daily. "Continually asking God to forgive us as we forgive others, Benedict suggests, warns us away from the vice of self-righteousness . . ." [159].

Unless your institution has a foundational commitment to a transcendent God, I have little confidence in its ability to sustain community in any meaningful sense. In an earlier time one might have made the case for the "community of scholars" being sufficient to foster a sense of meaningful and sustained community. My strong suspicion is that postmodernism and deconstruction have permanently burst that bubble.

What other "stakes" come with being "explicitly Christian"? Certainly the conviction that Jesus Christ is foundational, as the Apostle Paul suggests in I Corinthians 3:11. Certainly a commitment to what Jesus called the two greatest commandments, to love God with heart and soul and mind and strength, and to love neighbor as self. Certainly an attitude of respect and commitment and attention to the word of God as revealed in the Bible.

Isn't that enough, if we are to have a few things about which we are certain, rather than many? Belief in God, commitment to love that God, commitment to love neighbor, commitment to the son of God whose name we bear, commitment to take the Bible seriously. Isn't that enough?

It may be enough for Christian schools. I don't think it's enough for Mennonite schools. I think Mennonite schools also need to be unapologetically Mennonite. As staff at Mennonite schools we are, I hope and trust, dismayed at the evidence of rampant secularism that George Marsden reports and that we see all around us. But we are, I hope, also more than a little put off by that growing segment that enthusiastically embraces a Christianity that seems very unMennonite in its passionate embrace of God and country, its too-easy espousal of violence, its apparent enthusiasm for war. I think unapologetic Mennonitism must be part of the foundational stakes of our schools.

And what, you ask, does it mean to be unapologetically Mennonite? Let me begin by suggesting what it does not mean. It does not mean Mennonite ethnicity. It is not and cannot be a function of blood. Unless being Mennonite is an option every bit as open to the O'Reilly from New York or the Jackson from North Carolina or the Gonzalez from Texas or the Riungu from Kenya as it is to the Lapp from Lancaster or the Hess from Harrisonburg or the Waltner from Freeman, I'm not interested—and I trust you are not either. The issue isn't blood; the issue is distinctive theology and ethics.

I happen to think there are a lot of apologetic Mennonites around these days. One group of apologetic Mennonites feels that it is inferior to everyone else (at least to the Lutherans and Catholics and Presbyterians and Methodists and Episcopalians). Some of this may still be simply social insecurity. And we know that any humility generated by a sense of social insecurity is a false humility that dissipates when the social insecurity is corrected through education or experience. But some of this, I think, is just plain envy: the CEOs, the folks on the society page in the local newspaper, the beautiful people in our communities, tend not to be Mennonite. When these apologetic Mennonites are really honest, they would confess to themselves that they would much rather be beautiful people than be Mennonites.

There is another group of apologetic Mennonites that embodies the other meaning of the word apologetic; that is, offered in defense or vindication. These are the triumphalist Mennonites. They don't feel inferior to anyone. In fact, they feel superior to Lutherans and Catholics and Presbyterians and Methodists and Episcopalians and everyone else. They sometimes openly condemn the Mennonite commitment to humility as misguided. This may serve to justify (or rationalize?) an apologetic Mennonite tendency to build oneself up by putting others down.

When these apologetic Mennonites discuss the Reformation, for example, they often delight in exaggerated critique and caricature of the Lutherans, Calvinists, and Catholics. It makes them feel ever so much more holy and vindicated.

If what we are promulgating at our Mennonite schools is some form of this kind of apologetic Mennonitism, we should not be surprised to hear that those who choose not to share in that "vision" feel angry and alienated.

We need to find a better way, an unapologetic Mennonitism that is rooted in the affirmation and embrace of Mennonite distinctives—those few things about which we are certain. What are those distinctives? I offer five of those few Mennonite things about which we need to be certain:

The conviction that Jesus (in the Sermon on the Mount and everywhere else in the Gospels) meant what he said, and that he was talking to us.

The belief that there is a horizontal, as well as a vertical, dimension to salvation; that community actually matters in the life of the Christian.

The confidence that when Jesus told us to put away the sword, he meant what he said, and that he was talking to us.

The commitment to live more simply than we otherwise might.

The affirmation that Christians are indeed called to humility.

The paradox of humility

I have attempted to make the case for schools that are intentionally open, while at the same time being explicitly Christian and unapologetically Mennonite. But the ideal hasn't quite worked, has it? However compelling these two visions for Mennonite schools may be, the paradox persists, and we're not sure we can truly embrace it. If we have very strong stakes, how do we remain intentionally open? If we are passionately committed to openness, we're just not sure we want those stakes to be too strong. Miroslav Volf made the case for strong stakes in the face of openness, but doesn't that simply exacerbate the tension within the paradox? And even if it does make sense in our heads, how do we wrap our hearts around it? It would appear that we still have not found the key to embracing the tension; the key, if you will, to creating the bond.

I believe that we find the solution to this paradox of community in the words of the Apostle Paul in Ephesians 4:2. We will do it—we can only do it— "with all humility and gentleness, with patience, bearing with one another in love . . ." And so we confront a new paradox—the paradox of humility.

I need not remind you that humility is not in vogue right now in this country, though I'm not sure that it ever has been. After all, humility doesn't sell sneakers or muscle cars or subscriptions to the World Wrestling Federation channel or wars. It doesn't improve TV ratings; it doesn't encourage listeners on talk radio. But the Apostle Paul was right. It is absolutely essential—essential for creating the bond of community, essential for dealing with the paradox of the stretched curtains and strengthened stakes, essential for being a Mennonite Christian.

One of the paradoxes of humility is that true humility doesn't arise out of uncertainty; it is nurtured and sustained by certainty. Earlier I suggested that both types of apologetic Mennonitism are born of insecurity—a fundamental, perhaps even foundational, sense of insecurity.

Is it not possible for us to articulate and educate for a Mennonitism in which humility grows out of security rather than insecurity? I hope so, for it is only when we Mennonites are comfortable enough with who we are and *not* apologetic (in either sense of that term), that we will be sufficiently rooted, and therefore open enough, to listen to, learn from, and thereby effectively teach others.

I once heard John Esau, retired director for ministerial leadership in the General Conference Mennonite Church, say, "It is invariably when I feel most comfortable with being Mennonite that I am the most open and ecumenical." "Humility," says Parker Palmer, "is the virtue that allows us to pay attention to 'the other'" [*To Know As We Are Known,* p.108]. It is very difficult for persons who don't know who they truly are to pay attention to anyone else.

There is the certainty of knowing who we are that fosters humility, and there is the certainty of knowing who we are not. A few years ago, Gerald Biesecker-Mast of Bluffton College published an article in *Mennonite Life,* entitled "Jihad, McWorld, and Anabaptist Transcendence." In that article, Biesecker-Mast reminds us in modern terminology of the importance of what an earlier time called "the fear of the Lord." He notes that "the transcendent has too often been dangerously domesticated. . . . God has been conformed to human expectations rather than exceeding and challenging them" [6-7].

In so doing, of course, we presume to know truth absolutely, to become God, or at least to speak for God. From such a mistaken vantage point, it is all too easy and tempting to demonize, dehumanize, and ultimately destroy our opponents. Instead, writes Biesecker-Mast, "We are obliged to seek that transcendent God who makes us tremble, sears our tongues, and blinds our eyes" [7]. Now there's a prescription for walking humbly! Indeed, there is only one way to walk with God, and that is humbly. God is God, after all, and we are most assuredly not.

Finally, and perhaps most compellingly, there is the certainty of knowing Jesus Christ as the Son of God. Christ's message was all about humility—in word and deed. In Matthew 23:1-12, Jesus spoke directly about pharisaical behavior on the one hand, and servant behavior on the other.

Jesus didn't use only words. Consider his deed: "Let the same mind be in you that was in Christ Jesus, who, though he was in the form of God, did not regard equality with God as something to be exploited, but emptied himself, taking the form of a slave, being born in human likeness. And being found in human form, he humbled himself and become obedient to the point of death—even death on a cross" [Philippians 2:5-8, NRSV].

Gerald Biesecker-Mast has reminded us that we must walk humbly with God because that's the only way we can walk with God. Paul reminds us in Philippians 2 that we must walk humbly because that's the way God walks.

I suspect that right now some of you may be thinking, "Isn't this all just a little too easy, too neat? After all, Jesus was addressing his disciples. Paul wrote his letters 'to the saints who are in Ephesus' [1:1] and to 'the saints in Christ Jesus who are in Philippi' [1:1]. We may be church schools, but we are not the church. And you wouldn't believe some of the kids we've got running around in our classrooms. This so-called solution to the paradox of community is one thing if everyone in the community is committed to humility and forbearance. It might work in the church. But we've got students who can't even spell humility, much less practice it.

We've even got some colleagues who wouldn't recognize humility if they saw it."

In his recent book, *Walking With the Poor; Principles and Practices of Transformational Development*, Bryant Myers of World Vision addresses the issue of how we must encounter, not self-centered students at our Mennonite schools, but persons of different cultures, different nationalities, and, particularly, different faiths. Myers makes no apologies for his Christian faith. In fact, like Volf, he chides Christians for being unwilling to share that faith. But he makes some useful recommendations about when and how that faith is shared.

Of his many suggestions, I want to focus on two. Myers argues first that we must live "eloquent lives." "We need to do our work and live our lives in a way that calls attention to the new Spirit that lives within us. We need to relate to people . . . in ways that create a sense of wonder. We must seek a spirituality that makes our lives eloquent" [216]. "Live eloquent lives"—is that not a wonderful turn of phrase? Among other things, it reinforces the truth that values are caught, not taught. And if our lives as teachers do not radiate humility and love and forbearance, we can preach and teach about humility and community until we're blue in the face, but it will not register with our students, because there is no evidence that it has ever registered with us.

Myers is convinced that effective evangelism happens only in response to authentic questions. And "if people do not ask questions to which the gospel is the answer," says Myers, "we need to get down on our knees and ask God why our life and our work are so unremarkable that they never result in a question relating to what we believe and whom we worship" [210-211].

And then, when the question is asked and the encounter takes place, Myers makes a stunningly powerful argument for humility as the fundamental stance of the Christian. He suggests that we must approach all of these encounters with a "crucified mind." Myers borrows this phrase from Kosuke Koyama of Union Theological Seminary in New York ["'Extend Hospitality to Strangers'—A Missiology of Theologia Crucis," *International Review of Mission,* vol. 82, no. 327].

Myers writes of the temptation to slip into an unspoken attitude of superiority. Sometimes we are sure we know best because we are development pro-fessionals. Sometimes it is because we are educated or come from what we feel is a more sophisticated culture. Sometimes we fall into the trap of unknow-ingly judging another culture as not quite as good as our own. Sometimes it is because we have gotten caught up in the fact that we are Christians (or Mennonites?) and the others are not. Whatever the reason, this kind of attitude acts like a corrosive acid, eating away at our effectiveness in transformational development and Christian witness.

Instead of an attitude of superiority, Myers calls us to approach these encounters—with Muslims, with other Christians, with our faculty colleagues, with our students—not with crusading minds, but with the crucified mind of Christ. "The good news," after all, "is not ours to feel superior about or to use as a tool or a weapon. It is not our story; it is God's story."

Now in addition to being accomplished students of our disciplines, stimulating teachers on the pedagogical cutting edge, committee members, ticket-takers, class sponsors, home-room monitors, and who knows what else, you are being asked to live eloquent lives and demonstrate the crucified mind and the hospitable heart of Christ. And while it may be true that such lives and such minds and hearts will indeed allow us to stretch the curtains of our habitations even as we strengthen the stakes, we're just not certain that we have the energy.

The paradox of Christian discipleship

Before you get discouraged, remember that there is one final paradox. Paul suggests in Ephesians 4 that "each of us was given grace according to the measure of Christ's gift" [v.7]. And it was the resurrected Christ himself who said, "you will receive power when the Holy Spirit has come upon you . . . " [Acts 1:6-8]. In our stumbling, bumbling attempts to witness to the truth of the Gospel, to live eloquent lives, to embody the crucified mind and hospitable heart of Christ, there is a power beyond us at work for good. In our painfully human, often-subtly-selfish attempts to demonstrate love, there is a transcendent power of love working to bring healing and reconciliation. Paul writes in II Corinthians 4:7 that "we have this treasure in clay jars [earthen vessels], so that it may be made clear that this extraordinary power belongs to God and does not come from us."

We Christian disciples are therefore called to live in a delicious paradox. We must, on the one hand, constantly try harder—to be more loving, to be more eloquent, to be more humble, to be more compassionate, to be more open, to be more giving. And we must, on the other hand, and at the same time, willingly let go, willingly acknowledge that the power of that love, that eloquence, that humility, that compassion, that acceptance, that generosity, is a power that comes, finally, from outside of us, from a transcendent God, the true source of every good and perfect gift.

To live in this paradox is to strengthen the stakes while stretching the curtains. To live in this paradox is to be poised for creating the bond, for building community in our churches, our homes, our classrooms, our schools. To live in this paradox is to be both certain and humble. To live in this paradox is to keep our balance as we inch our way along that narrow footpath of Christ. May it be so!

Dale Schrag, North Newton, Kansas, is Director of Church Relations at Bethel College and Secretary of the Higher Education Council of the General Conference Mennonite Church.

Book Reviews

Women Without Men: Mennonite Refugees of the Second World War, by Marlene Epp. Toronto: University of Toronto Press, 2000.

Reviewed by Rachel Waltner Goossen

This is a haunting, gracefully written history of the experiences of the approximately 8,000 Mennonites who arrived in Canada in the late 1940s and early 1950s in the aftermath of famine, war, and dislocation from their homes in the Soviet Union and uncertain years as refugees in postwar Germany. Although the book gives primary attention to women and children who found their way to Canada, one chapter discusses the approximately 4,000 Mennonites who migrated to the Paraguayan Chaco before many of them, too, immigrated to Canada in the 1950s.

Women Without Men is a compelling story of mass immigration as well as a feminist reinterpretation of this chapter in Mennonite history. Epp, herself a second-generation Canadian, began this project as a doctoral thesis at the University of Toronto. In addition to mining primary sources at Winnipeg's Mennonite Heritage Centre and the Centre for Mennonite Brethren Studies, she interviewed 34 Mennonite women and men from Ontario, Manitoba, Alberta, and British Columbia about their immigration experiences. Additionally, she drew from oral history interviews conducted in the early 1950s by Russian Mennonite immigrant and historian Cornelius Krahn. The resulting book—which probes the Mennonites' wartime traumas, impoverishment, refugee status, and efforts to adjust to a new land—is an important addition to both immigration and Mennonite historical scholarship.

The title *Women Without Men* aptly describes the book's subject of primarily fragmented, female-headed families on the move. Most of the Mennonites who in the 1940s trekked westward from their homes in the Ukraine to Germany and then to North or South America underwent separation from family members. Tens of thousands of Mennonite men—husbands, brothers, sons—had been exiled or murdered during Stalin's "Great Purges" in the 1930s, killed while participating in German self-defense leagues during World War II or, later, repatriated to Soviet territory from postwar German occupation zones. Drawing on wartime German surveys of Mennonite villages in the Ukraine as well as the records of the Canadian Mennonite Board of Colonization and other sources, Epp reports that Mennonite women immigrating to Canada outnumbered Mennonite men by a 2:1 ratio. Most of the men who had survived and managed to immigrate were either elderly or in their late teens.

In Epp's analytic framework this dramatic imbalance in the gender ratio is not an incidental but rather a central facet that helps to illuminate many dimensions of the immigrants' life experiences. It also provides a point of departure from conventional wisdom. As Epp points out, North American immigration studies have usually taken male experience as normative since immigrants, historically, have often been either single young males or men "leading" their families to new lands.

Epp's subject is compelling, for while the Mennonite women she describes encountered many of the same problems common to immigrants in other places and other times, they also encountered significant differences. They were vulnerable to sexual abuse and exploitation, issues rarely documented in standard immigration studies. As "heads of households," these women also had more opportunities to exert leadership and to develop a range of practical skills, from driving wagons to negotiating bureaucracies, as well as performing heroic deeds such as saving others' lives, than they might have in more normal circumstances. Yet even in their own late-in-life reminiscences, these women—perhaps conditioned by a cultural framework that tends to regard single or widowed women as weak or burdensome—did not generally describe their experiences in terms of courage or heroism. Epp explains, "After years of turmoil and instability, most immigrants were eager to be settled and secure, which also meant fitting in as much as possible" (186).

Their lives before coming to Canada had been extraordinarily complex, and "fitting in" to established norms of Mennonite family and church life proved difficult. Epp explores many dimensions of their experiences. Of the 35,000 Mennonites who fled the Soviet Union alongside the retreating German army in 1943 approximately 23,000 died or disappeared along the way or were eventually repatriated to Soviet lands. The 12,000 Mennonites remaining in Europe (who then migrated to Canada or South America) had endured much. Some were survivors of torture and rape or had entered into sexual liaisons with "protective" German officers. Among these were women who bore illegitimate children or underwent abortions. Many lost loved ones through traumatic circumstances and thereafter carried burdens of guilt when they compared their own survival with the fate of friends and family members.

Later, in Canada, these women, some widowed and many with fatherless children, would attempt to reconstitute family structures. Remarriage was one avenue toward "normalcy." Yet, as Epp explains, many of these former refugees were unsure what had happened to their spouses, and most General Conference and Mennonite Brethren churches in Canada prohibited remarriage of persons whose marital status was uncertain. As a result, formulating acceptable family lives—even in relatively comfortable Canadian communities—remained difficult. Established Mennonite conferences and congregations offered substantial help to the immigrants through private charity and mutual aid institutions. But the knowledge that the immigrants' wartime experiences had very likely included "bribery, stealing, lying, sexual encounters, and of the men, military service" contributed to social divisions between established Canadian Mennonites and the newcomers they aimed to assist (169-70).

The strongest sections of the book are the first several chapters, which focus on the European experience. Later chapters, which follow chronologically the immigrants' adjustments to Canada, are intriguing but deal briefly and inadequately with some topics, especially acculturation processes such as acquisition of the English language and entry into formal educational institutions.

But this is a small quibble. In probing such sensitive wartime subjects as rape, violence, and escape, Epp offers a revisionist perspective on Mennonite migration. For example, memories of female refugees have rarely been taken into account by scholars assessing migration. Here, however, women's recollections of almost unspeakable acts of terror in occupied Berlin are placed alongside the more familiar story of MCC-sponsored North American relief workers' efforts to help thousands of refugees escape. The traditional focus on MCC relief workers, Epp argues, has tended to shift attention away from the Berlin refugees but nevertheless has "given the story the status of myth in Mennonite history" (67).

Epp's interpretive handling of the women's assessment of their own stories and accomplishments is subtle. She acknowledges that the women who had to assume roles as heads of their families viewed their own circumstances as tragic aberrations. Even when women banded together to create stronger communities for survival, such as in *Frauendorf* in the 1940s Paraguayan colony of Neuland (called "womens' village" because all 147 adult residents were female), Epp reports that physical hardship characterized this agricultural community from the very beginning.

A primary goal of this book is to lift up stories in which Mennonite women remember with pride their savvy and skill as survivors. And, indeed, readers will find much to admire in the unforgettable drama of their journeys. But the troubling dimensions of their stories are never far from the surface. For scholars who know what a struggle it can be to achieve balance in characterizing their subjects (in this case "heroines" or "victims"), and for general readers who prize complex storytelling, Epp's nuanced history is a "must" read.

Rachel Waltner Goossen, Topeka, Kansas, is a history professor.

Transcending: Reflections of Crime Victims, by
Howard Zehr. Intercourse, PA: Good Books,
2001.

Reviewed by Gordon Houser

Our nation is in the midst of a debate about the
death penalty. Too often ignored in this debate are the
victims of violence. A new book by Howard Zehr, who
teaches in the conflict transformation program at
Eastern Mennonite University, Harrisonburg, Va., helps
remedy that neglect.

Five years ago, Zehr published a photo-interview
book, *Doing Life: Reflections of Men and Women
Serving Life Sentences* (Good Books, 1996), which
drew attention to people hidden from our eyes.

His new book, *Transcending: Reflections of Crime
Victims,* also reveals subjects we don't usually give our
attention. It includes 75 artistic photographs of people—
including at least two Mennonites—who have endured
violence done to them or loved ones. Their gripping stories make it difficult to put the book down.

In Part II, Zehr offers his own analysis in
"Victimization and the Obligations of Justice." He draws
on his more than 20 years of pioneering the field of
restorative justice to outline what victims of violence
experience.

He writes, "The experience of violence, then, calls
into question our most fundamental assumptions about
who we are, whom we can trust, and what kind of
world we live in." He goes on to describe victims' journeys toward meaning, honor, vindication, and justice.

Unfortunately, the criminal justice system in the
United States does not help people in these journeys.

Zehr quotes author Judith Lewis Herman: "If you set out to design a system for provoking intrusive post-traumatic symptoms, one could not do better than a court of law."

Restorative justice has two basic principles, writes Zehr: "First, the ones harmed—victims and survivors—should be central to justice . . . Second, the question of offender accountability should focus on encouraging offenders to understand and, to the extent possible, take responsibility for that harm."

Zehr writes that "victims' voices should be heard, in all their diversity and complexity, even when they are difficult to hear, even when we are uncomfortable with their positions." This book honors those voices by including them, with their faces.

An important part of the healing for many of these courageous people is their coming to forgive. Conrad Moore, whose son was murdered, writes: "Forgiving was our only opportunity to exercise control in the whole process. When you forgive, you actually have some power. It's like a sign of relief."

Every congregation, at least, should have this important book.

Gordon Houser is a writer and an editor of The Mennonite, *living in Newton, Kansas.*

God's Healing Strategy, An Introduction to the Bible's Main Themes, **by Ted Grimsrud. Pandora Press, U.S., 2000, and** *How to Understand the Bible,* **by David Ewert. Scottdale, PA: Herald Press, 2000.**

Reviewed by John W. Miller

The Bible is not faring very well in modern culture, the Old Testament in particular. Ellen Davis of Virginia Theological Seminary recently stated that many experience the Bible as so "complex and morally problematic" that it has ceased functioning as Scripture in the mainstream churches she is acquainted with.

These two volumes are notable attempts at addressing this issue.

Ted Grimsrud's book proposes that the Bible be read as a story about "God's healing strategy." The story begins in Genesis 1-11, where we are told of a decision within the heart of God.

In grief and anger at human perversity and violence, God unleashed a destructive flood—but then changed his mind and decided that the only way forward was to heal creation through nonviolent "gentle, everlasting love."

"This choice of God to pursue healing without coercion is basically the story of the rest of the Bible—culminating in the work of Jesus Christ," Grimsrud writes. The remaining chapters of his book are an attempt at fleshing out this story.

David Ewert addresses the same issues in a different way. He writes about a variety of topics he thinks might be helpful for ordinary Bible readers.

Among them are the "pre-understandings" we bring to Bible study, guidelines for interpretation, languages, and translations, diverse cultural contexts, and unifying themes.

"Progressive revelation" is an important concept when reading the whole Bible, he stresses. The Bible is much like a two-act drama, he suggests, with the Old Testament and New Testament. Both acts reveal God's love and plan for saving the world, but there are important differences.

Israel was the chosen instrument of God in the Old Testament, yet on the whole, "Israel failed in carrying out its mission to the nations," he writes. A major reason for this failure (in his opinion) was Israel's ethnocentricity. In the new Israel (the church) "all racial and national boundaries are transcended."

Both books raise important issues for discussion. To obtain his version of the biblical story, Grimsrud passes over features of the narrative that are discordant with his thesis. An example would be Genesis 9:1-6, a pivotal text in which God authorizes the descendants of Noah to use force in protecting human beings made in his image.

This text is the background of New Testament teachings on the same subject (for example, Romans 13:4). Is this not also part of "God's healing strategy"? Does God work only through "gentle" nonviolent love?

Ewert's emphasis on "progressive revelation" is helpful, but bifurcating the church and Israel also raises questions. Was pre-Christian Israel as ethnocentric and ineffectual in its witness to nations as he suggests? Did it not assemble scriptures upon which Christians are still dependent for their witness to the nations?

These are important books deserving a wide readership.

John W. Miller, Kitchener, Ontario, is a retired professor.

Tasting the Dust, by Jean Janzen. Intercourse, PA: Good Books, 2000.

Reviewed by Lori Matties

Jean Janzen's poems are spare and tight, but the richness of her imagery takes my breath away. The poems are about the earth and how she occupies it; about nature and how it receives us; about history and how it reaches forward to us; about life and death and how they call us beyond our understanding. The book is divided into four sections, each one introduced by a poem describing a painting by the Dutch artist, Vermeer. The paintings are of women alone in a room, each one suspended in a moment of activity; opening a window, pouring milk, reading a letter, weighing pieces of gold. Like Vermeer's paintings, Janzen's poems reach out beyond themselves to something we yearn for and yet fail fully to comprehend.

In Part I, "Window Facing South," the poems are about the valley where Janzen has made her home and the mountains that overlook it. Janzen celebrates the land's fertility, the mountains' beauty, and provisions of water for the valley. Comparing the "necessity" of the one and the "grace" of the other, she asks, ultimately, "Where is home?"

Part II, "Window Facing North," is an exploration of human relationships. "Our stories are too big/ for our bodies," she writes. Our lives, dreamlike, circle around "that non-dream/ we try to imagine, around which/ my poems circle—," from which we come and which we try all our lives to understand.

Images of Holland, Mennonite martyrs, and Italy are the subjects of the poems in Part III. In these poems we are treated to a gallery of descriptions of paintings: those of Dutch painters, including Vermeer, a stunning poem likening Van Gogh to the suffering servant in Isaiah 53, and the Italian frescoes of Fra Angelico. Like those in the rest of the book, these poems pull the reader through the painting to the artist's imagined intent or captured moment and to Janzen's, and our, apprehending of it.

Part IV returns closer to home, with poems remembering the lakes of Janzen's childhood and recording the death of her ninety-five year old mother. In the final poem, "Tasting the Dust," she returns to the garden where the sweat of her husband's toil is his restoration. But the garden also tells

the story of dust, an origin
so deep and dense, it rose
like fire to make the mountain,

a narrative of tumble
breakage from its sides,
the wet roar of ages

under the slow beat of the sun.

In her repeated use of natural elements such as dust, air, leaves, Janzen grounds us in the paradox of earth and spirit. Though the dust covers everything, it is the air, she says "into which we sail,/ breath by dusty breath,/ toward a different shore." In the end, though, "it is the air/ itself, which finally claims us, / drawing our last exhalations/ into its reckless burning, this air/ which we have borrowed since/ our first

stunned gasp." What we try to capture is transient,
always in motion so that we can only glimpse it.
Even so something "is saved somewhere" and in our
longing for that something that is saved,

> what/ we finally hold in our empty hands
> is what we glimpsed—a memory
> of beauty and sweetness like a secret home,
> where, when we enter, someone
> calls us by a new name.

For me, what finally makes these poems attractive,
beyond the exquisite use of language, is Janzen's cap-
turing of both the beauty and the frailty of earthly
existence, framed by an apprehension of something
more enduring. Here are words worth staying with,
images that both delight and invite further thought.

*Lori Matties lives in Winnipeg, Manitoba, and is the edi-
tor of* Sophia *magazine.*

The Hammer Rings Hope: Photos and Stories from Fifty Years of Mennonite Disaster Service, by Lowell Detweiler. Scottdale, PA: Herald Press, 2000.

Reviewed by Joseph A. Sprunger

Mennonites have become known as a people who respond in the name of Christ to disasters. Every North American Mennonite has probably heard of Mennonite Disaster Service (MDS) and either has participated or knows someone who has participated in an MDS response. So an amply-illustrated book with many color photographs on its history should have several kinds of utility, surely another Mennonite expectation! Lowell Detweiler spent 12 years as MDS Director and two years preparing this book. Peter J. Dyck, who wrote the forward, and a number of other Mennonite leaders are quoted either briefly or at length in the narrative.

Detweiler tells the story of MDS by compiling interesting pieces on specific MDS responses and how both participants' and victims' lives have been influenced. The narrative begins with the tornado that hit Hesston, Kansas, in 1990 and features the family of Kirk and Jean Alliman, then president of Hesston College, whose home was destroyed. It is a moving story about suffering and caring in the same Mennonite community that was the birthplace of MDS about 40 years earlier. Other stories include the first MDS (then called MSO/Mennonite Service Organization) response, a flood in Wichita, Kansas. John Diller of Hesston, Kansas, served as the first coordinator. Major responses chronicled in the book include the Palm Sunday tornadoes (1965), hurricanes Agnes (1972) and Andrew (1992), and the Red River floods (1997) in the Dakotas and southern Manitoba.

This broad story line is interspersed with chapters on organizational origins and development. In the late 1940s young veterans of Civilian Public Service (CPS) reflected in their Sunday school classes on their role in the post-war setting. When circumstances called for help, they acted on their belief that service to the broader society was as relevant in a time of peace as in an earlier time of war, when such service was obligatory rather than voluntary. It is implicitly clear that the roots of MDS reached into the ferment of the CPS experience for spiritual, social, intellectual, and organizational nourishment.

The key to the development of MDS occurred when local, regional, and national Mennonite leaders recognized and nurtured the organizing potential in local disaster responses without smothering them. Capable local people initiated these responses among their neighbors and fellow church members in a context that already valued unpaid service. Detweiler traces how larger Mennonite structures such as Mennonite Central Committee (MCC), with headquarters in Akron, Pennsylvania, provided broader organizing and governance assistance. In order to protect the broader structures as well as to empower local and regional initiatives, MDS and MCC have fashioned a fluid and mutually supportive relationship over the years. The valuable role that MDS has played both in the life of the church and for communities in need is a strong argument that this relationship with MCC took the right turns.

The organizational development of MDS has evolved into a regional and local system of volunteers. They use modern electronic and communication technologies to track disasters, communicate where and when workers are needed, and manage the disaster response. One telling illustration (p. 143) shows older volunteers in a computer class as a part of MDS leadership training. Church youth groups also bring a vital presence to many MDS projects. This story of MDS reaching into congregational life may contain lessons for both other congregations and church structures.

As with much writing by Mennonites about Mennonites, one finds a tendency to downplay or totally ignore public policy and its implications. One sidebar describes how the U.S. tries to control flooding by constructing massive river levees, while Canada builds ring dikes around properties that need protection (p. 89). By identifying the differences in public policy, analysis is implied but not presented. The book also describes MDS-related efforts to help victims deal with official agencies and the household and business implications of having their lives so seriously interrupted by disasters. However, who suffers how much from disasters is very much influenced by public policy decisions in advance of actual disasters. Such a book on direct service to people in need may not be the appropriate forum for such a discussion, but that discussion should have a relevant forum somewhere. Just as Mennonites expect their financial resources to be used wisely, their resource of influence, enhanced by the work of MDS, should also be used to positively impact the same people whom their direct assistance helps.

This volume has many stories about people who have suffered in disasters and people who have been helped. The reader learns of stories of responses where MDS volunteers worked with racial and other minorities, intentionally focusing on the poorest victims least likely to be served. The strongest stories describe relationships built in the experience of helping others. Many MDS responses have fostered new relationships between traditional white Germanic-origin Mennonites offering help to people from minority groups whose lives have been wounded by disaster. MDS workers often experience growth and fulfillment which they did not know they either needed or could have hoped to gain. With Saint Francis, MDS volunteers learn that it is in giving that we receive.

This book can serve to initiate conversation with friends and other visitors about who Mennonites are and what they do in the world. For those who have participated in MDS responses, the book recognizes their efforts either directly or indirectly and thereby offers an opportunity to recall and relate their experiences. Numerous stories could be used as examples in sermons or other presentations. The book has numerous photographs, many brief sidebar stories, and understandable timeline charts (pp. 176-180) which show the significant responses by region, state, and province. I sense that the book was written primarily to edify people already committed to and practicing the ideals of MDS. It serves this purpose well.

Joseph Sprunger lives in Metuchen, New Jersey.

Anabaptist Visions for the New Millennium: A Search for Identity, edited by Dale Schrag and James Juhnke. Kitchener, ON and Scottdale, PA: Pandora Press and Herald Press, 2000.

Reviewed by John A. Lapp

In an article in the January 2001 *Mennonite Quarterly Review* on "Mennonites in the Year 2000," I rather presumptuously listed 25 significant books published last year by or about Mennonites. I was sure to miss some important ones. The book reviewed here is a very important one I missed.

I did mention the conference held at Bethel College last June where the papers in this volume were first presented as one of the significant meetings of the year. The Fransen Family Foundation should be congratulated both for inspiring the conference and underwriting the publication of the papers.

I sometimes shy away from reviewing books with so many authors. All 28 presenters are included in this volume. While there is some expected unevenness, each presentation is relevant, and more than a few are exceptional.

The papers are divided into seven sections, which provide a clue to the coverage: A Search for Identity; Theology and Church; Engaging the World; New Voices; Worship; Mission and Evangelism; and the two summaries. The presenters included the inevitable professors but also students, pastors, a businesswoman, and at least six definable ethnicities.

In a conference on "Anabaptist Visions" there would have to be references to Harold Bender's classic statement of 1944. What is refreshing is that the revisioning done in other times and places was not repeated at the Bethel conferences. All the presenters tried to be constructive theologians both in theory and in practice.

The opening essay by Brenda Martin Hurst is a powerful appeal to repudiate patriarchy and become a "one-another" community where "all are humbled by kneeling to wash the other's feet *and* all are honored and respected by having their feet washed as well." Martin Hurst recalls her Lancaster County family where at age 16 the males received cars and the females hope chests. Unhappily, that continues to be a metaphor for the treatment of males and females in the church.

The theme of gender equality recurs regularly in these visions for the new millennium. Paul Keim, in his eloquent conclusion, observes that "there is something wrong with Mennonite theology that keeps men from relating to women with honor and respect . . . that leaves many women in our families and congregations wounded and wanting."

A second theme introduced in the second essay by Karl Koop is locating the root of a newly stated vision of the triune God. Many of the subsequent essays underline and expand Koop's theme: "When we know, love, and worship this God, and when we are, as a collective body, engaged in mission and service, our identity will emerge and our vision will become clear."

Arnold Synder, Duane Friesen, Marlene Kropf, John Rempel, and Cynthia Neufeld Smith particularly apply the vision of God in revitalized public worship. A number of essays deal with discipleship and

peace. Each suggests a renewed emphasis on God's
grace in human relationships and an understanding
of the church that engages the world both in the
ordinary and the extraordinary.

Several of the essays are literary gems. Vern
Rempel's "The Spirit and Barbed Wire" wonderfully
evokes church life on the Great Plains. John D.
Thiesen uses Shakespeare's "To Bury, Not to Praise"
to challenge the use of the term "Anabaptist" in
describing contemporary Mennonites, a point of
view with which I strongly agree.

Paul Keim, with wit, humor, and sobering perspective, has one of the most succinct but hopeful summaries that I've ever read in "What's Wrong With
Being Mennonite?" His suggestion that we think less
in terms of Anabaptist vision and more in terms of
Anabaptist consciousness is a helpful way to look
ahead at the restructuring of the entire Christian
movement in North America.

The Baptist theologian-ethicist Glen Stassen from
Fuller Seminary provides the other deeply encouraging summary statement. This friendly outsider
focused on the blessings he received at the conference and blessings that the Anabaptist tradition has
contributed to the larger Christian cause:
Peacemaking practices under the Lordship of Christ,
Christ-centered biblical hermeneutics, churches with
definition and commitment, visible churches that
make a difference. That was the agenda for the past
five centuries. It is the essential agenda for the 21st
century.

I highly recommend this volume, which will surely spark fresh thinking. I can envision Sunday school

classes and small groups spending six to eight sessions making the teaching here relevant to our congregations and to ourselves.

John A. Lapp, Akron, Pennsylvania, is a former executive secretary of Mennonite Central Committee.

Calling God "Father": Essays on the Bible,
Fatherhood, and Culture, by John W. Miller. New
York: Paulist Press, 1999, second edition.

Reviewed by Valerie G. Rempel

In *Calling God "Father": Essays on the Bible,*
Fatherhood, and Culture, John W. Miller has updated
and added to the collection of essays first published
under the title *Biblical Faith and Fathering: Why we*
call God "Father" (Paulist Press, 1989). The new edition contains some minor revisions, a new essay, and
some bibliographic updating. It is organized into four
sections: Theoretical Considerations, God as Father
in Biblical Tradition, Human Fathering in Biblical
Tradition, and Contemporary Issues. There is also a
concluding chapter and appendices.

Miller's goal in republishing this collection is, he
writes, the same as it was 10 years ago. The author
wants to draw attention to "omissions and distor-
tions" in the ongoing discussion of biblical patriarchy
and the language used in reference to God. Miller is
concerned about what he sees as the "refutation of
'the "Father" in God' in contemporary feminist the-
ologies" and its implications for the maintenance of
father-involved families (xvii). Chapter 10, a new
essay, is particularly directed toward this end.

What propels Miller's work is his belief that there
is a fundamental harmony between the Bible and
psychoanalytic theory when it comes to the importance of fathering and the impact of fathers on
healthy child development. Miller sees a link
between Israelite faith in a father-god (in contrast to
the mother-gods or son-gods of other eastern tradi-

tions) and the development of a strong pattern of
father-involved families. Christianity, arising out of a
Jewish context, also emphasized the importance of
good fathering, and Miller goes on to suggest that
there has been great benefit to all cultures which
have embraced the idea of God as a gracious father.
Since God as "Father" provides the ideal model for
human fathering, feminists who seek to downplay
the importance of this name and the role it represents risk doing further harm to modern families and
particularly to children.

Miller begins his defense of "the 'Father' in God"
with an examination of how the two-parent family
came about in history and the changes this development brought to human culture. Father-involvement,
he suggests, could only arise as humans began to
understand the role that males play in human repro-
duction. This led to the creation of specific male-
female pair bonds and ultimately to the father-
involved family. In his view, fathering is "the defini-
tive cultural artifact that lies at the foundation of all
other cultural achievements" and is the primary fac-
tor in distinguishing humans from other life-forms
(17). Yet, because human fathering is a cultural construct, it is inherently more fragile than the biological bond that shapes the relationship of mother and
child, and is thus more at risk.

Miller argues that the very name Yahweh implies
fatherhood and that throughout the Old Testament
God's actions demonstrate the nature of God's
fatherhood. Patriarchy, he suggests, is best understood as good fathering and not simply masculine
power or supremacy. This is fundamentally impor-

tant for both males and females, who need a healthy father in order to develop secure gender identities.

Miller is aware of earlier criticism directed toward these essays and tries to refute the critique that his focus is too directed toward fathers and sons. He attempts to argue that it is also girls and women who need both a strong father figure in God and good human fathering in order to develop healthy identities. That may be so, yet many readers will object to Miller's strong reliance on Freudian psychoanalytic theory to develop this point. This is a major weakness of the book and betrays a rather narrow and dated understanding of human developmental theory. In addition, Miller's reluctance to fully grapple with the implications of the New Testament's reorientation from biological family to spiritual family is problematic. It is not enough to say that Jesus and Paul were both single and therefore naturally drawn to the community formed by the early church. Surely this New Testament orientation and its concern for widows and orphans have much to offer a society beset by rising divorce rates and single-parent households.

Because these essays grow out of lecture material and previously published articles, they are somewhat repetitious. Nevertheless, Miller writes in a clear, organized, and generally accessible fashion. Readers seeking to understand the biblical arguments in support of God as "Father" should find this a helpful resource.

Valerie G. Rempel is part of the Mennonite Brethren Biblical Seminary in Fresno, California.

Dangerous Elements, by Sarah Klassen. Kingston, ON: Quarry Press, 1998.

Simone Weil: Songs of Hunger and Love, by Sarah Klassen. Toronto, ON: Wolsak and Wynn, 1999.

Reviewed by Ann Hostetler

Since the publication of her award-winning collection of poetry *Journey to Yalta* in 1988, Sarah Klassen has become an increasingly important voice on the contemporary Canadian Mennonite literary scene. As editor of *Sophia*—a magazine by and for Mennonite women—and *Women and Violence,* published by the Feminist Caucus of the League of Canadian poets, Klassen is also actively involved in several sites of production of Canadian women's literature. Her introduction to *Siolence: Poets on Women, Violence, and Silence,* places her at the center of a network of feminist and spiritually grounded writers who attempt to bridge the gap between activism and poetic contemplation. Many of the poems in her recent collection *Dangerous Element*s reveal Klassen's interest in artistic collaboration: two poems respond to art installations by Canadian women artists; the ambitious long poem "Born Again: Excerpts from a Woman's Space Journal" has been set to music by Canadian composer Linda Schwartz; and six other poems in the collection have either been set to music or have inspired musical composition.

Dangerous Elements and *Simone Weil: Songs of Hunger and Love* reveal a new maturity in Klassen's work and underscore her importance as one of Canada's leading Mennonite poets. These two books, although thematically linked, are in some ways opposites, showing Klassen's poetic range. While *Dangerous Elements* is expansive in its attempt to synthesize the complexity of postmodern subjectivity with questions of faith, *Simone Weil* is an intensely focused work, based on meticulous research and a keen sensitivity to Weil's artistry that explores the consciousness of this twentieth-century spiritual martyr. Yet both collections are linked by the poet's underlying quest to lay bare the ambiguities of the martyr's search for an absolute faith, which is the legacy of martyrdom in the Mennonite story, and to reinterpret these themes in contemporary settings and terms.

The poems of *Dangerous Elements'* six sections are firmly rooted in the present moment among the artifacts of contemporary life. The poems are set in cafes, kitchens, restaurants, art galleries, a shoe museum; they bring the reader along on bird-watching expeditions and tours of historical sites; they move from the streets of Winnipeg to the streets of Lithuania. Yet shards of history, like the splintered edges of complex fractures, threaten to erupt through the flesh of the present. From its opening suite centered on bird-watching to its final poems written after the engravings of Jan Luyken for *Martyrs' Mirror,* the work in *Dangerous Elements* is concerned with the problematic of looking, of watching, of artistic observation and interpretation. For instance, in a poem from the first section, two friends watch pelicans gather on the rocks as they tour Massacre Island, site of a bloody confrontation between settlers and Indians; in the last section Klassen explores both the martyrs' experiences and Luyken's artistic dilemma as he etches the images of faith: "He tries defining/ faith: should it be modest or bold,/ reasonable, fervent, fanatical? He's drawn to the plain/ homeliness of bound hands/ and feet, a stretched wrist . . . " The reader is inexorably drawn, through these meditations, into exploring the "dangerous elements" that our comfort-oriented contemporary society would have us keep at the periphery of vision. The poems in *Dangerous Elements* succeed admirably in linking the concerns and legacy of the Anabaptist martyrs to the quest for an aesthetic and spiritual appreciation of existence. My major criticism is editorial rather than literary: the volume is almost overfull and could perhaps have been more successful as two separate books.

While *Dangerous Elements* threatens to explode out of focus with its complexity and richness, *Simone Weil: Songs of Hunger and Love* is focused, spare, and memorable. The three sections—"Hunger," "God Exists Because I Desire Him," "We Can Only Cry Out"—provide a formal structure that suggests the organization of a musical composition. The poems, written in a lyric voice imaginatively Weil's, employ a language that is plain, spare, disarmingly simple, and provocative. Klassen's ability to get inside the mind of the writer, her accurate research and her attunement to Weil's sensibility effectively present both an appreciation and a critique of this unusual prophetic writer whose demanding spiritual commitment rivaled the absolute devotion of the Anabaptist martyrs. Both gave their bodies in a consummation of their faith. Again, in this volume, Klassen links the Anabaptist themes of her earlier writing with the larger human story of suffering and faith. Klassen's poems are a valuable appreciation of Weil's unique contribution as a spiritual writer and living witness to faith. They are also highly accessible and refer to many of Weil's published essays and biography, all of which makes this book a good introduction to this challenging thinker.

No collection of contemporary Mennonite literature will be complete without both of Klassen's recent volumes, which make a significant contribution to the shape of Mennonite writing today.

Ann Hostetler, Goshen, Indiana, is a professor and writer.

Film Ratings and Video Guide, 2001

The following capsule reviews rate movies which have shown in theaters (some are foreign films with very limited release) from an adult perspective on a scale from 1 (pathetic) through 9 (extraordinary), based on their sensitivity, artistry, integrity, and technique. These listings include a number of movies from the second half of 2000.

Along Came a Spider— Another psychological thriller about a cop-doc. This time he's trying to find a senator's kidnapped daughter. Implausible. (2)

America's Sweethearts— A total waste of talent. Light fare which goes down hill. When the premiere of a movie will make or break the studio, strange things happen. (2)

Amores Perros—A sensational dissection of Mexican life. Three stories occasionally interact and examine the well-off, the working class, and a street person. Relationships to dogs play a big part in this electrifying triple-layer of life and suffering. (8)

Angel Eyes—A hodge-podge yarn about a Chicago cop and the man whose life she saves. (3)

Anti-Trust—A fun but goofy thriller about a brilliant young software programmer who is hired from his own garage lab by a mega-corporate giant and placed at the top. But why? (5)

Bandits—A funny, bickering trio of bank robbers make for an entertaining heist flick. Echoes of "Bonnie and Clyde," but much more flat at spots. (7)

Blow Dry—A bouncy, sassy yarn, set in a small British town in the middle of a national hairstyling contest. Becomes quite entangled. Sags. (4)

Bread and Tulips—A near-perfect Italian romantic comedy about a housewife who "accidentally" takes a vacation from her inappreciative family. Very delightful midlife crisis film, spoiled only by the ending. (7)

Bridget Jones' Diary—A winsome tale about a 32-year-old London lass who wants to be slim, have a caring mother, and find Mr. Right. Quite amusingly executed. (7)

Captain Corelli's Mandolin—Yarn about a mandolin-strumming Italian officer during WWII who falls in love with a Greek woman. Story could have worked, but actors are miscast and chemistry is nil. (3)

Cast Away—A FedEx systems engineer is stranded on a remote, uninhabited island in the South Pacific. A remarkable solo performance by Tom Hanks. Tries for deep meaning, but greatness eludes this story of survival. (7)

Chocolat—Charming but heavy-handed little story about a beautiful woman whose scrumptious candies bewitch a small French town. Delicious tale, fine acting, but manipulative

sermonizing about tolerance. (6)

The Claim—Three strangers come to visit a California mountain town, dominated 20 years after the Gold Rush of 1849 by a very wealthy, very harsh man. A man with a past. Great scenery. (6)

Crazy/Beautiful—Top drawer, as flicks about boy/girl go. Wealthy, spoiled white girl. Hispanic boy. She's rebelling, he's conforming. An interesting love story in a cross-cultural setting. (7)

Crouching Tiger, Hidden Dragon—Visually spectacular, poetically mesmerizing, this historical fantasy set in China with a touch of King Arthur stands in a class of its own. The story's a bit convoluted and the drama lags at times, but it is not to be missed for its visual magnificence. (7)

The Curse of the Jade Scorpion—A funny (by spells) Woody Allen movie about a hapless insurance investigator who ends up pursuing himself. Would be stronger if Allen could figure out how to accommodate real passion in his story alongside that trademark angst. (6)

The Deep End— Exquisitely realized thriller about a mother who tries to keep her teenage son from getting into trouble. Mesmerizingly effective. (7)

Diamond Man—An offbeat picture with a homemade feel, following a spent salesman from store to store as he tries to train the reckless, brash young man hired to replace him. Has fresh energy and originality in a marvelous story. (8)

Divided We Fall— Poignant and funny story, set in a small Czech town during WWII. A Gentile couple reluctantly give shelter to a Jewish concentration camp runaway, right under the nose of the occupying Germans. Excellent. (8)

Domestic Disturbance— Disappointing melodrama about a father who worries about his son, now that his ex-wife has married someone he doesn't quite trust. Too over the edge. (3)

Don't Say a Word—An engaging, crackling thriller about a psychiatrist who has to extract a six-digit number from a severely-traumatized patient in order to save his own daughter from menacing kidnappers. (6)

Dr. Seuss' How the Grinch Stole Christmas— Misfires. Jim Carrey's overacting, the less than lovable characters, and the extravagance of the visuals all add up to a flat melodrama. (3)

Enemy at the Gates—Set in 1942 Stalingrad, this movie begins with grandscale cliches, but closes with an above-average contest between two hardboiled snipers. (4)

Everybody's Famous— Involving Flemish film about father-daughter relationships. Dreams of showbiz for the father; lack of self-confidence for the daughter. Offbeat and charming. (7)

Faithless—An unrelenting drama about an affair and its impact on a disintegrating marriage. Ingmar Bergman wrote the screenplay—in his confessional, excellent, but typical take on marriage. Nearly suffocating, but unforgettable. (7)

The Fast and the Furious—Dazzling tale about street racing in L.A. A newcomer tries to infiltrate. Interesting characterizations. (5)

Finding Forrester—An old writer who peaked early now hides from the world. A 16-year-old basketball player and secret writer befriends him. The chemistry grows, each helping the other. A wonderfully written and acted movie. (8)

Ghostworld—A superbly-etched portrait of two misfit teenagers, best friends, unscathing in their view of

what life is not. Through their own unkindness, they become involved with a middle-aged misfit with similar sensibilities. Offbeat but excellent. (7)

The Gift—A Gothic thriller about a widowed mother of three in a small Southern town whose psychic abilities include seeing a murder. Above average for its genre. (4)

The Golden Bowl—With barely a pulse, this slow, mannerly drama set in the early 1900s in Europe looks at a wealthy family. (4)

Hardball—Warmhearted collection of cliches about coaching a sandlot baseball team because of a gambling debt. (3)

Heist—A crook who wants to quit, gets double-crossed. Great writing, strong directing, and superior acting by Gene Hackman and Danny De Vito. Somehow the curves in the road add less than expected to the heft of the project. Still, quite good. (7)

House of Mirth—The hypocrisies of turn-of-the-century New York society are skewered through this finely-acted tale of the fall of a socialite. (7)

Joy Ride—A really enjoyable, really scary near thriller. Two brothers at odds, and a girlfriend, on a cross-country trip, stalked by a mysterious, menacing trucker who doesn't appreciate their CB pranks. (7)

The Last Castle—A court-martialed general is sent to a military prison where, after some heroic heavy breathing, he leads an uprising. Lacks credibility at every turn. Contrived. (2)

Legally Blonde—A pleasant, feel-good diversion about this blond sorority girl who, compelled by her uppity boyfriend, goes to Harvard Law School to beat him at his own game without, like, ever giving up her, like, Cosmo Girl principles, like, ever. (6)

The Luzhin Defense—Understated romance between a brilliant, withdrawn chess genius and the devoted woman he attracts in 1929 Italy. Could have been superior instead of merely worthwhile. (6)

Malena—A beautiful school teacher arrives at a wartime, seaside Sicilian town. Local folks are scandalized by the gossip they themselves invent. But an adolescent boy, whom she never notices, loves her and follows her everywhere. A dazzling story, framed by the tragedy of war. (7)

Memento—This movie attempts the unusual feat of telling the story backwards, even though the lead character has a condition where he can only remember things for 15 minutes or so. A man seeks his wife's murderer. Strikingly achieved in riveting dread. (7)

Men of Honor—A gritty, somewhat uneven confrontation, based on a true story of an African American Navy diver and the bigot who trains him. Old-fashioned look at valor. (5)

The Mexican—A too droopy, too violent yarn about a bagman for the mob, his girlfriend, and a kidnapper. Funny at moments. (4)

Miss Congeniality—Charming in spite of a lot of dead weight, thanks to Sandra Bullock's buoyant portrayal of a tomboyish FBI agent who goes undercover as a beauty pageant contestant. (6)

The Others—Above average tale of a mother raising her two children in a haunted house while her husband's away at the war. (4)

Pavilion of Women—An American missionary in '30s China falls in love with a middle-aged woman. (4)

Pearl Harbor—Sags from the sheet weight of too big a story, too big and old-fashioned a movie. Bloated and hackneyed account of the attack on Pearl Harbor and subsequent events. (2)

The Pledge—This uneven film follows a retired cop who's determined to find the killer of a little girl. (5)

Pollock—A top-notch little movie about a big problem. This excellent portrait of Abstract Expressionist painter Jackson Pollock etches the tension between the pursuit of unblinking truth on the canvas and a chaotic personal life absorbed with shutting out the truth. (7)

Proof of Life—The wife of an American engineering executive who's been kidnapped in a Latin American country tries to secure his freedom. She hires a rugged negotiator to help. At times thrilling, at others bland. (5)

Quills—An overwrought film about the Marquis de Sade's last years, shut away for his evil deeds. The attempt to delineate evil from evil results in an unsatisfactory and melodramatic tale. (3)

Remember the Titans—This warm fuzzy about race relations and football is worth seeing, in spite of being sentimental and manipulative. Denzel Washington is always fun to watch. Here he portrays a black high school football coach with much to overcome. (6)

Riding in Cars with Boys—A bright young woman is trapped by a teenage pregnancy into marrying a loser. A tender mix; stronger acting and tighter pacing could have made it a classic. (7)

The Score—An intelligent, well-crafted movie about an old pro and a brash young con man, teaming for the heist of a lifetime. Chemistry of acting and script is suspenseful and superb. (7)

Serendipity—A light dessert, but enjoyable. A guy meets the woman of his dreams, but immediately loses her. Will they ever meet again? Cliches, cliches, but charming nonetheless. (6)

Sexy Beast—A menacing, frightening crime flick about a thug who lores a former associate back to London for one last crime. Well done, but dark, violent, and savage. (6)

Shrek—A marvelously energizing computer-animated tale about a gruff but kindhearted ogre. The script is hilarious, as is the animated acting. Adults will enjoy it as much as kids. (8)

Snatch—An abrasive, violent caper movie, constantly out-of-breath. Too much. (2)

Songcatcher—A feisty musicologist finds in the mountains of Appalachia music worth catching. Romance and intrigue add to the sparkle of the music. A wonderfully realized small film. (8)

Spy Game—A superb, grand spy story, coupled with a small, all-in-the-inner-office spy caper, makes for one of the better espionage films of recent years. Will the old guy, on the day of his retirement, risk it all to save a rogue? (7)

State and Main—A Hollywood movie crew invades a quiet New England village. Very funny and sad as both the predictable and the unanticipated unfold. (7)

The Tailor of Panama— A disappointment. A sleek British spy on a slippery slope tries to land on his feet. False tips about the Panama Canal set off myriads of intrigue. Sadly, this film has a double life—one part tightly woven, one part unraveling. (4)

Thirteen Days—Sadly, this drama which tries to recreate the behind-the-scenes detail and atmosphere during the Cuban missile crisis in 1962 seems self-conscious and wooden. (4)

A Time for Drunken Horses—A poignant portrait of a Kurdish adoles-

cent trying to provide for his sisters (his mother's dead, his father far away). Captures pathos and survival determination very well. In Kurdish and Farsi. (7)

Traffic—An outstanding provocative look at the tough world of drug traffic. An opus of myriad settings and storylines, intertwined, saved by fine acting and superb directing. (8)

Unbreakable—A lone survivor of a train wreck tries to discover why in this dark, supernatural misfire. (3)

Under the Sand— Outstanding portrait of a middle-aged woman, struggling to act normal after her husband disappears at the beach. Charlotte Rampling's best role. Eloquently implicit. (7)

Vertical Limit—A melodrama with breathtaking mountain-climbing sequences. A brother and a sister try to grapple with the death of their father.

The photography's great, the character development a bit unbelievable. (4)

The Wedding Planner—A pleasant romantic comedy. A wedding planner tries to balance her career with an unexpected romance. (6)

What Women Want— A pleasing, light comedy about a male chauvinist who, through an electrical accident, acquires the ability to read women's minds. He learns more than he expected to. (5)

The Widow of St. Pierre—A beautiful, flawed story. Too transparent in its propaganda. Set in 1850 on the French Canadian island of St. Pierre, the town awaits the arrival of a guillotine to execute a fisherman who committed a brutal murder. The Captain's wife tries to intercede. Well done. (7)

With a Friend Like Harry—A riveting psychological thriller about a man who attaches himself to an unsuspecting family by claiming to be an old classmate of the husband. Taut and full of surprises. (7)

You Can Count on Me— An outstanding smallish film about a sister and her brother, both now adults. Superb writing, fine acting, and excellent directing combine for an unforgettable story about two siblings trying to find common ground and some sort of healing. The timing of the conversation and the nuances are just right. (9)

Merle Good of Lancaster, Pennsylvania, is a writer, dramatist, publisher, and a co-editor of this volume. He has been reviewing films for nearly 30 years.

Our Sponsors

Formed in Christ, Transformed to Lead

EASTERN MENNONITE SEMINARY offers nine programs of study, including master's degrees in divinity, religion and church leadership.

EASTERN MENNONITE SEMINARY

A Graduate Division of
Eastern Mennonite University

For 25 wonderful years, we have welcomed intelligent questions.

"We found the most sensitive presentation of Amish life at The People's Place." — **National Geographic Traveler**

Among our features, open year-round to the public:

- **"20 Questions: A Discovery Museum for All Ages,"** an interactive museum developed around the 20 most asked questions about the Amish and Mennonites. Highlights differences and similarities among modern and Old Order groups.

- Newly Revised **"Who Are the Amish?,"** a dramatic three-screen documentary about the Amish.
  "The photography was lush, the narration intelligent."
  — **The New York Times**

- **The People's Place Book Shoppe**, specializing in books about the Mennonites and the Amish. More than 500 titles.

- **The People's Place Quilt Museum**, featuring exhibits of antique Amish and Mennonite quilts.

- The Village Pottery, featuring the finest work by more than a dozen Mennonite-related potters and ceramic artists.

25 Wonderful Years

Route 340, P.O. Box 419
Intercourse, PA 17534
(In the heart of the
Old Amish settlement.)
9:30 a.m.–5 p.m. daily.
Closed Sundays.
800/390-8436
www.thepeoplesplace.com

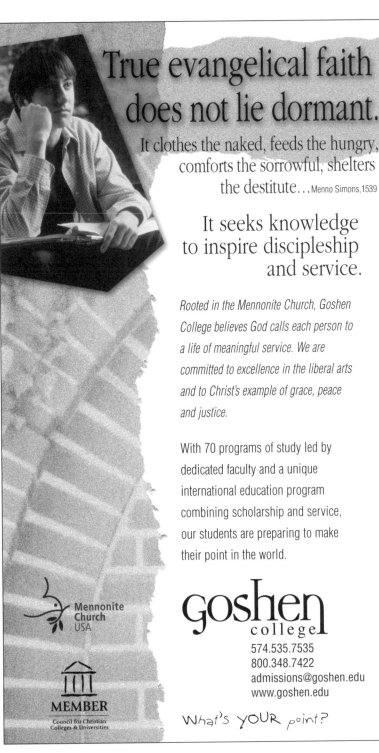

One-Stop Resource!
Books about the Mennonites

- Biography
- Fiction
- History
- Peace/Justice
- Children's Books
- Family Life/Parenting
- Marriage
- Poetry/Music
- Cooking
- Meditation
- Women's Studies
- Humor
- Quilts/Decorative Arts
- Missions
- Grief
- Gift Books
- Leadership

Reliable. Readable. Reputable.

Cumulative Indexes

(Includes 1998, 1999, 2000, and 2001
collections of
What Mennonites Are Thinking)

By Subject

abortion – '99, p8

academic entrepreneurs – '98, p69

accountability – '98, p64; '98, p108; '01, p30; '01, p119; '01, p176

affluence – '98, p68; '01, p4

aging – '99, p125; '99, p119; '01, p4

agriculture – '01, p9; '01, p54

Amish – '98, p14; '98, p154; '99, p28; '99, p106; '99, p271; '01, p54; '01, p87

Anabaptist – '98, p29; '98, p115; '98, p135; '98, p252; '99, p24; '99, p115; '99, p135; '99, p138; '99, p171; '99, p231; '99, p268; '99, p280; '00, p48; '00, p159; '00, p242; '01, p54; '01, p263;'01, p270

the arts – '98, p44; '99, p27; '99, p142; '01, p20; '01, p168

baptism – '98, p135

Barth, Karl – '01, p160

believers church – '99, p161

Ben's Wayne – '99, p27

Bender, Harold S. – '99, p230; '99, p256; '99, p;268

Benedictine – '00, p159

Bible, biblical – '99, p7; '99, p238; '00, p52; '01, p145; '01, p168; '01, p253; '01, p267

Bruderhof – '99, p46

business entrepreneurs – '98, p69

calling – '01, p30; '01, p224

Canada – '98, p102; '00, p4; '01, p246

capital punishment – '99, p8

celebrations – '01, p41; '01, p110

charismatic – '99, p83

children – '00, p59

Christmas – '01, p41

the church – '98, p60; '98, p69; '98, p115; '98, p139; '99, p25; '99, p86; '99, p134; '99, p138; '99, p163; '99, p168; '99, p183; '99, p230; '99, p232; '99, p246; '00, p41; '00, p180; '01, p12; '01, p82; '01, p140; '01, p157; '01, p176; '01, p263

church discipline – '98, p60; '99, p56; '01, p27; '01, p119; '01, p126

church global – '98, p26; '99, p13; '99, p82; '99, p168; '00, p41; '00, p90; '00, p137; '01, p12; '01, p49; '01, p152; '01, p157

church membership – '00, p9

church splits – '00, p9; '00, p16

Civilian Public Service – '98, p40

collecting books – '01, p145

Colombia – '01, p49

comfort – '01, p152

commitment – '00, p159; '01, p49; '01, p119; '01, p126; '01, p224

community – '98, p60; '98, p92; '98, p233; '98, p242; '99, p24; '99, p86; '99, p106; '99, p155; '99, p163; '99, p246; '00, p33; '00, p118; '01, p30; '01, p49; '01, p119; '01, p224

compassion – '01, p27; '01, p49

confession of faith – '99, p5

conflict resolution – '98, p214

conquest – '00, p52

conscientious objector – '98, p20; '98, p40; '01, p46

conservative – '98, p238; '99, p7; '99, p21

Constantine – '99, p156; '99, p244

consumerism – '98, p109; '98, p130; '99, p10; '01, p41

contraception'99, p35

courage – '98, p105; '98, p139; '01, p20; '01, p30; '01, p46; '01, p152

creation, nature – '98, p14; '98, p32; '98, p137; '01, p9; '01, p54; '01, p131

creativity – '01, p20

crime – '01, p251

cross-cultural – '98, p4; '98, p168; '99, p149; '99, p197; '00, p23; '00, p33; '01, p9; '01, p12; '01, p157

culture and faith – '98, p135; '98, p242; '99, p151; '00, p150; '01,

By Scripture Reference